The Logic of Tao Philosophy
道家哲學的邏輯

The Logic of Tao Philosophy
道家哲學的邏輯

Revised Edition
(November 18, 2021)

Wayne L. Wang, Ph.D.

Helena Island Publisher
2021

Published by

Helena Island Publisher
1717 Clemens Road
Darien, Illinois, USA 60561

Copyright © 2013 by Wayne L. Wang
All rights reserved.

All rights reserved. No part of this book may be used or reproduced in any manner whatsoever without written permission. No part of this book may be stored in a retrievable system or transmitted in any form or by any means including electronic, electrostatic, magnetic tape, mechanical, photocopying, recording, or otherwise without the prior permission in writing of the publisher.

16 15 14 13 / 10 9 8 7 6 5 4 3 2 1

Printed in the United States of America
[November 18, 2021]

Wang, Wayne L., 1944 -
The Logic of Tao Philosophy /by Wayne L. Wang;
(A Searching for Tao Series)

[Also available in the Kindle eBook]

Cover Artwork: Ceramic "Tao 道" by Shu Hwang
        Photographer: Lekki Chua
        [Permission by the Artists]

DEDICATION

To
Those who have dedicated efforts to uncover the mystery of Tao, those who have been perplexed about this little book, and those who have tolerated the author's long solitude hours in completing this work.

Nature Independence Series

Nature Independence Series is to provide the theoretical basis and ability to establish new Laozi philosophy. All editions are bilingual, a few with English-only versions.

1. **The Tao Te Ching: Bilingual Translations**
   English-only version: Tao Te Ching: An Ultimate Translation
2. **The Myth of Taoism:** Analyzes the chapters of the *Tao Te Ching*
3. **The New Laozi Philosophy**
   English-only version: *The Logic of Hegel, Buddhism, and Taoism*
4. **Wisdom of Laozi in Simple Words**
5. **Awakening of Taoism (A Chinese Don Quixote Novel)**
   English-only version: Chaos of Taoism
6. **The Logic of Tao Philosophy（2015, revised）**
7. **The Story of Tao: a Graphic Novel Vol. I (English)**

The reference and this book are available at www.amazon.com as eBook, paperback, and hardcover. The book abstracts are in https://dynamictaos.com.

One

I am One
I am only One
I am but One

But I am One.

CONTENTS

CONTENTS 7
PREFACE 15

    The Purpose of the Book..17
    The Principles of Tao 18
    Interaction Model and Linguistic Model 19
    Ambiguous Description of Reality.......................................21
    New Interpretation..22
    Our Translation of the Tao Te Ching..................................22
    Acknowledgment 23

PART I: A SYSTEMATIC MODEL I
CHAPTER I INTRODUCTION..1

    Is there Logic in Tao Philosophy?..3
    Historical Commentaries...4
    Our Journey...4
    The Principle of Tao Philosophy..7
    A Language-independent Principle 8
    Breaking-Out of an Endless Loop 9
    Think like a Chinese? 10
    A Perennial Philosophy 10
    Lao-tzu proclaims his Principle 11
    Refocusing the Mysteries of Tao..12
    A Systematic Model 13
    Structure of this Book 14
    A new Translation and a Graphic Novel...........................14

CHAPTER II THE PRINCIPLE OF TAO..............................15

    Brief Summary of the First Chapter 19
    Basic Concept of Heng 21

  ANALYSIS OF THE FIRST CHAPTER...22

    1. Heng Tao and Heng Name 23

  2. Wu and Yu as Conventional Objects 23
  3. Heng Wu and Heng Yu as Realities 24
  4. Same Time and the Same Tao 25
  5. Mysteries of Tao as Profound 26

 THE BASIC ARCHITECTURE 26

  Actualities and Manifestations 28

 THE PRINCIPLES OF TAO PHILOSOPHY 30

  The Principle of Oneness 30
  The Principle of Complementarity 31
  The Principle of Equivalence 32

 A SYSTEMATIC MODEL 33

PART II 35
CHARACTERISTICS OF THE MODEL 35
AND 35
NEW INTERPRETATIONS 35
CHAPTER III THE LOGIC OF TAO PHILOSOPHY 37

 THE LOGIC OF TAO PHILOSOPHY 39

  The Model Architecture 40
  Actualization and Objectification 41
  Interactions between Objects 41

 THE COMPLETE LOGIC MODEL 42
 THE INTERACTION MODEL 43

  Relational Structure of Actualities 45
  The Principle of Complementarity 45
  Reality is Indivisible 46
  Reality as Relational Proposition 47
  Actualities reflect the same Principle 48
  Interference of superimposed Objects 49
  Many-to-Many Relationship 50
  Complementarity is not Self-Contradiction 51
  The Principle of Interactions 52
  The Tai-Ji Symbol 53
  Reality Vectors and Coordinates 55

Many-Worlds Representation *58*
THE LINGUISTIC MODEL 59
   Simple and Complex Concepts *60*
   Quantification of Concepts *61*
   Quantification of Objects *63*
   Quantification of the Actualities *63*
   Logical Description of Reality *65*
   Fuzzy Logic *66*
   The Third World *66*
   Language Problem *67*
   The Images in Our Brain *69*
SUMMARY OF THE LOGIC 70

CHAPTER IV CHARACTERISTICS OF THE TAO LOGIC 72

THE CHARACTERISTICS AT EACH LEVEL 74
   The Absolute Reality and God *74*
   Characteristics of Actualities *75*
   Actualization *76*
   Illusions *77*
   Trinity *78*
   The doctrine of Two Truths *78*
   Objectification *79*
   Characteristics of the Objects *80*
   The Objects Have Limited Reality *80*
   The Objects obey Formal Logic *81*
   Objects are Social Products *82*
   Objects are Non-Being *82*
   Objects create Illusion *83*
   A Many-to-Many Relation *83*
THE INTERACTIONS OF THE OBJECTS 84
   The Law of Interactions as Te *84*
   Tao, Te, and Chi form a System *85*
   The Harmonization Forces *86*
   Teleological Forces *87*

  MANIFESTATIONS ARE EQUIVALENT..88
   Opposite Ways to the Same Goal 89
   To Incite the Opposite..89
   Tao moves the Opposite..90
   The One and the Many...90
   The Tao Te Ching is not Self-Contradiction.......................91
  DUALISTIC FALLACIES 93
  CREATIVITY 94
   Creativity by Groups 95
   Being and Becoming...96
  LANGUAGE EVOLUTION 97

CHAPTER V NEW INTERPRETATIONS **98**
  RELATIONSHIP OF WU AND YU 99
   Source of Traditional Misinterpretation...........................100
   Complementarity of Wu and Yu 101
  WU-WEI AND YU-WEI 102
   Recovering the Earlier Views 103
   Demarcation of Wu-wei and Yu-wei..................................104
   Traditional downplay of Yu-wei 104
  THE MYSTERIES OF TAO 105
   Complementarity of Objects 106
   Realities are unambiguous 107
   Spontaneous Transformation..108
   Omnipresence of Tao..109
  COMMON LOGICAL ERRORS 110
   The Root of Tao Philosophy 110
   Softness and Tenderness...111
   Cyclic Transformation is Illusion 112
   Actuality is not in the Middle...113
   Illusion of Time...113
   Wisdom and Knowledge 114

THE PROCESS PHILOSOPHY OF TAO 116
   Multi-step Actualization *116*
   Levels and Groups in the Tao Te Ching *119*
   Five Levels *119*
   Five Groups *120*
   Tao as Philosophy of Organism *120*
THE THREE LEVELS OF THINKING 121

CHAPTER VI SUMMARY **123**
   TAO AS A COMMON PHILOSOPHY 125
   THE PRINCIPLE OF ONENESS 127
   MODERN SCIENCES 130
   RELIGIONS 131
   A NEW INTERPRETATION OF TAO TE CHING 133
   A PARADIGM SHIFT 134

APPENDIX A: TRICHOTOMY OF TIME **135**
   STRUCTURE OF PSYCHOLOGICAL TIME 136
   HOLISTIC CHANGES IN TIME 138

APPENDIX B: KEYWORDS **140**
   IN THE FIRST CHAPTER OF THE TAO TE CHING 140
   KEYWORDS IN THE LOGIC MODEL 142
   OTHER KEYWORDS 146

REFERENCES **147**
INDEX **149**
ABOUT THE AUTHOR **155**

Figures

Figure 1 Basic Architecture of Tao Philosophy   27
Figure 2 Interaction Model Architecture   40
Figure 3 The Actualization Process 44
Figure 4 The Tai-ji Symbol 53
Figure 5 Thought Space and Reality Vectors   56
Figure 6 Complementarity of Two Hemispheres   69
Figure 7 Multi-step Process Philosophy   117
Figure 8 Psychological Time   137
Figure 9 Time Change   138

Modification Notes

We make use of Print-on-Demand (POD) technology to print this book. We can then provide continuous updates to the contents of this book. The copy you order online is always the most up-to-date version. The revision date is shown on the copyright page. Significant simplifications are made in December 2014 and February 2015.

03/26/2015	Add references to Rene Guenon: The Multiple States of the Being
04/11/2015	Clarification on the terms used: body, soul, and spirit.
	Actuality is translated as 實象, to pair with Object as 物象.
05/04/2015	Comments based on Positivism Comte added.
11/20/2015	Major overall revision and Chinese Translation

This version is dated: November 18, 2021.

Revised Edition

This revised edition contains major rewritings of the overall text. This edition was used as the reference for a Chinese translation of this title into Chinese by Mr. Lu Ying Tang.

The Logic of Tao Philosophy

Preface

The significant problems we face cannot be solved at the same level of thinking we were at when we created them.
Albert Einstein

Like other oriental traditions, Daoism has been misunderstood and misappropriated in a variety of ways, and like China itself has been the object of both the best and worst kinds of free-ranging fantasy.

J. J. Clarke
The Tao of the West

We all love mysteries. In more than 2000 years, Chinese scholars and many Western scholars have been convinced that the *Tao Te Ching* 道德經 is mysterious beyond normal philosophical reasoning; therefore, the *Tao Te Ching* is open for diverging interpretations. Consequently, historical interpretations end with irreconcilable paradoxes and self-contradictions.

Our fascination with Tao is not based on what we know about Tao, but on what we cannot comprehend about Tao. The principle of Tao has been formally declared unfathomable and unknowable. Therefore, some Chinese scholars heralded Tao as a unique Chinese intellectual treasure that has no equivalence in the West. In the West, few have treated the *Tao Te Ching* as a genuine "philosophical" text, as observed by Ames and Hall, "The *Daodejing* is a profoundly "philosophical" text, yet it has not been treated as such." (Ames 2003)

Boldly said, we are about to change such a well-rooted historical view with systematic analysis. We shall present the principle of Tao based on the *Tao Te Ching*. Most people will frown upon any systematic study of the *Tao Te Ching*; therefore, any such attempt will face a formidable tradition of mysterious speculations about Tao. It will be difficult to convince anyone that there is a clear principle in Tao philosophy. Nevertheless, we shall show that it is an authentic philosophy of nature and Lao-tzu is a logical philosopher.

Our conclusion is completely contrary to the prevailing view and is a significant and accidental discovery. We started this project without any anticipation of such a result. However, after a long period of analysis, it has become clear that there is a clear principle and a clear logical structure in Tao philosophy. We shall carefully provide convincing evidence for the reader.

The Purpose of the Book

The purpose of this book is to convey enough foundation for a proper understanding of the principle and logic of Tao philosophy.

We shall show the logic of Lao-tzu based *solely* on the *Tao Te Ching*. Lao-tzu's logic has been blurred in the historical interpretations. In other words, logic cannot be derived from historical interpretations, since the historical interpretations have not been executed logically. Our alternate approach is to dismiss most historical commentaries as "authoritative," and return to the textual analysis of the *Tao Te Ching* itself to recover its logic and principle. The logic is depicted fully in the first chapter of the *Tao Te Ching*.

We can firmly say that the historical commentaries have indeed distorted the principle of Tao. We are aware that such a claim is extraordinary and will certainly be challenged by many traditional Tao philosophers. However, the evidence is overwhelming in our favor to support our conclusions. The principle will be self-evident and the words of Lao-tzu are not mysterious when we understand the principle of Tao.

The Principles of Tao

The myriad things follow an order in the phenomenal world. Tao philosophy describes that order as the natural, spontaneous, harmonious order of the universe. Tao philosophy is a Philosophy of Nature that calls Tao the proper interrelations among the myriad things. It is difficult to describe this order directly since its sole characteristic is Oneness.

We may summarize the principle of Tao as the Principle of Oneness, the Principle of Complementarity, and the Principle of Equivalence. We can see these principles in the interrelations of the myriad things in the phenomenal world. With these principles, some of our traditional views on Tao can be re-affirmed, but many other speculations are unwarranted. The most important is that our way of thinking should obey the same principles of Tao to be realistic and practical, so as not to fall into self-contradiction.

These principles are based on the Tao Te Ching. However, we can see the same principles in many other philosophies and must conclude that Tao philosophy is not a Chinese-only philosophy. The principle is common among the East and West philosophies.

In Western philosophy, the model will show how the objects should participate in the forms of Plato. The similarity of Tao philosophy to Parmenides, Heraclitus, and Plotinus is astonishing. The principle of Tao is also consistent with many modern Western philosophical observations, such as by Schelling, Kant, Bradley, and Whitehead, etc. In modern sciences, the principle is reflected in the quantum complementarity of the two opposite natures of particle and wave. In Eastern philosophy, there is a basic similarity with the Buddhist philosophy. All are based on the Oneness of nature.

Interaction Model and Linguistic Model

The logic model is based on the first chapter of the *Tao Te Ching*. This systematic model provides a pathway to recognize Lao-tzu's logical path and identify his concepts rigorously and logically. The model may appear intuitive and heuristic, but it shares the methodology of sciences and other philosophical inquiries.

The model shows a logical way to describe the manifestations of reality, without falling into dualistic fallacies. Tao itself cannot be directly described, but our model will describe how the *principle* of Tao works in the phenomenal world. We assign various names to and use language to describe the myriad things. The words are parts; the manifestations of Tao are whole.

Our model can resolve the most fundamental problem in the East and West philosophy: the model is a study of "the parts and the whole.".

There will be two aspects in the whole model. The first aspect is the *conceptual relations* between the parts and the whole. The parts are different conceptual representations of the whole. However, these parts often become fragmented in our habitual thinking. We show how these fragmented parts are integrated to maintain the wholeness in an *Interaction Model*. The second aspect is the relation between the concepts and the language we use to represent these concepts. We show how we can describe concepts with language in a *Linguistic Model*.

With these two models, we can show how Lao-tzu uses words to describe manifestations of Tao. This is the logic of Tao philosophy. The purpose of these models is only to steer our minds on the proper path. Our model is not new; similar models have been implicitly used since ancient times.

What is new in these models is our use of more precise language to express such models. The two models are similar to scientific models.

The analytic results may appear unfamiliar to some readers, but they are the mathematical representation of the familiar yin-yang complementarity shown in the Tai-ji Diagram 太極圖. Our key result is the logic that Lao-tzu uses to describe the reality of nature. If we analyze the *Tao Te Ching* with this logic, the verses will stand true by themselves, without relying on the model.

Ambiguous Description of Reality

Philosophers are fully aware that language is insufficient to describe reality. The words of Lao-tzu appear ambiguous, so we have to show that such ambiguity is a natural result of logical thinking. We can show that the words that depict a reality will appear ambiguous due to the nature of our language, not the nature of reality. The reality will always be unambiguous.

The words of Lao-tzu are "vague, self-contradictory, and indeterminate," but they logically reflect the reality of Tao. We can show analytically the logical structure of our linguistic description of reality.

This is an important discovery of our model. It is a very important paradigm shift in our understanding of Tao. Now we have to take Lao-tzu's ambiguous words seriously because what he describes is not ambiguous. We can no longer dismiss Lao-tzu's words as incomprehensible paradoxes, and cannot speculate randomly; instead, we have to change our approach to interpreting the *Tao Te Ching*. We can follow this model to search for the logic behind these ambiguous words.

New Interpretation

We identified the principle of Tao in this model analysis. This principle is the *ultimate* target for our interpretation of the *Tao Te Ching*. We may follow this principle to eliminate the apparent contradictions in the interpretations and our interpretations will be coherent and free from random speculations.

We may also minimize the difficulty in the translations. A genuine principle is language-independent, so we can describe the same *principle* of Tao equally in any language. The language is different, but the *principle* expressed will be the same.

The logic model was first published as a Chinese article, 道家哲學的邏輯, in the *Tamkang Journal of Humanities and Social Sciences*, pp. 1-32. The contents have been expanded in this book for the general public.

Our Translation of the Tao Te Ching

Our English translation is published as a companion to this book: *Tao Te Ching: An Ultimate Translation*. The *Logic of Tao Philosophy* and the *Ultimate Translation* represents a definite step forward in our understanding of Tao philosophy.

We shall also publish a Graphic Novel: *The Story of Tao (Volume I)*, as a more relaxing way of representing the Tao philosophy in Graphic Novel format.

Acknowledgment

This work represents a major milestone in our study of Tao philosophy. It spanned more than a decade. The author would like to take this occasion to express thanks to many friends who have provided direct and indirect support for this project during its long history. The author would like to recognize Profs. Chen Gu-yin 陳鼓應, Tong Lik-Kuen 唐力權, Prof. Lin Yi-cheng 林義正, and Ho Hsiu Hwang 何秀煌. They have impartially extended their supports to an unknown amateur at the early stage of my efforts. However, the project has had many major changes since and they may be unaware of the final work presented here. The author also thanks the editors and the anonymous reviewers of the article in *Tamkang Journal* to make the logic model available for the academic public.

The author thanks Mr. Lu Ying-tang 呂應棠, Kan Tiong Siong 簡忠松, Su Jin-long 蘇金龍, and Yu-san Chen 陳玉山, for their discussions related to the model. For this book, the author thanks Mark Ristich and Helena Wang, who have reviewed the early drafts and provided many comments. The author also likes to thank Mr. Don Dudycha and Mr. Mattie van Rooijen for their comments.

The revised edition has been greatly modified during the translation of this book into Chinese by Ying-Tang Lu.

Part I: A Systematic Model

執今之道，以御今之有，
以知古始。是謂道紀。

It is by holding the Tao of today to observe
the phenomena of today, that
We come to know its ancient beginning.
This is the Threads of Tao.

(From the *Lao-tzu*, Chapter 14)

Chapter I
Introduction

Only if Oneness exists,
What we discuss here is true,

The significant problems we face cannot be solved at the same level of thinking we were at when we created them.

Einstein

Although the Tao Te Ching has five thousand characters, what "threads through them" is Oneness.

Wang Bi

The chapter will recount our efforts in the search for logic in the *Tao Te Ching*. Traditionally, the *Tao Te Ching* and the *Book of Changes* 易經 have been regarded as the most important foundation of Chinese philosophy. Paradoxically, this high regard is not based on our understanding of these books, but on our inability to decode these books.

Most East and West scholars believe that the foundation of Chinese philosophy cannot be logically described, and thus the world is divided into two incompatible systems of thought. Chinese thought also becomes a questionable philosophy.

However, we are about to change this history!

The famous German philosopher Georg Hegel (1770-1831) and many other Western philosophers simply proclaim that China does not have a philosophy. Recently, the contemporary French postmodern philosopher Jacques Derrida (1930-2004) also comments that during his China visit in 2001, "China has no philosophy, but only thought." Such comments immediately invoke again the question of the legitimacy of Chinese thought as a philosophy. Therefore, it is important to re-visit the nature of Chinese philosophy.

Logic is the foundation of philosophy. Isn't it perplexing that an "illogical" *Tao Te Ching* can have so much *philosophical* influence in China? Are we convinced that ancient Chinese philosophical thinking is without logic?

Historically, except for very limited logic discussions and debates by Hui-shi 惠施 (370-318 BCE), Gongsun Long 公孫龍 (320-250 BCE), Hsuen-tzu 荀子 (325-238 BCE), and Mo-tzu 墨子 (470-391 BCE), there has been little discussion of any logic in ancient China. None of these discussions point to the *Tao Te Ching* as a logic platform.

Chapter I Introduction

The first introduction of Western logic was done in 1905 and 1909 by Yan Fu 嚴復 (1895-1921). There have been also some analyses of Chinese logic by modern philosophers, such as Hu Shih 胡適 (1891-1962),[1] Zhang Dongsun 張東蓀 (1886-1962), and Jin Yuelin 金玉霖 (1895-1988), etc. However, overall we have not been able to identify a clear system of Chinese logic.

Is there Logic in Tao Philosophy?

Virtually all Chinese thinkers are comfortable with a Tao philosophy that does not have a clear logic. Many will even readily dismiss any claim of Western logic in Tao philosophy and some will even revolt against any discussion of "logic" in Tao philosophy. The terms, "Logic" and "Tao philosophy," have become a well-established oxymoron, and the title of this book [The Logic of Tao Philosophy] will appear as a joke to most Tao scholars.

However, against such prevailing belief against any logic in Tao, we shall change this status quo and reveal the logic of Tao philosophy. This book will identify the logic of Tao philosophy and will restore Lao-tzu as an authentic philosopher. This will completely change the traditional views about Tao philosophy.

---

[1] Hu Shih, *The Development of the Logical Method in Ancient China*, Paragon Book Reprint Corp, New York (1963),

This may be the first book in history dedicated to *The Logic of Tao Philosophy*. It is an important "archeological" discovery and is a direct challenge to the traditional views on Tao philosophy. As we shall see, our conclusion is likely to be valid.

Historical Commentaries

We cannot rely on historical commentaries, since many were made from different backgrounds and for different purposes. These historical interpretations have created the current ambiguities and contradictions. If we follow the same historical interpretations, we will not be able to solve the problems that were created by these interpretations. Therefore, we shall treat these historical interpretations with great caution, and will do not regard them as "authoritative."

Occasionally, there are consensuses behind various historical interpretations and reflect the glimpses of a common truth. Therefore, we refer to such historical interpretations. In principle, we have chosen to search for the principle directly in the text of the *Tao Te Ching*.

Our Journey

In 1999, I decided to look at the *Tao Te Ching* as a personal homage back to society. This journey started with a simple curiosity: Why is the *Tao Te Ching* so difficult to interpret? After some understanding of the principle, the question becomes: "Is it truly beyond any systematic analysis?"

Chapter I Introduction

After I analyze the principle, I ask "Why do so many questions remain unanswered for such a long time?" Now, the final problem becomes: How I can share the logic of Tao philosophy with others?

Our initial interpretation reflects some similarities between Tao philosophy and the non-dualistic nature in modern sciences. This was published in 2004 as the *Dynamic Tao and Its Manifestations*. Many observations in that book are still valid, but the notion that "Yu comes from Wu" is incorrect.

Soon afterward in 2005, we were able to show the basic and the proper duality nature of Wu and Yu in the *Basic Theory of Tao Philosophy*.[1] That article marks a "scientific turn" in our search path, some principle emerges from the *Tao Te Ching* itself and thus we can start to search for a consistent principle behind the verses. We started a long search journey along with The *Basic Theory of Tao Philosophy*.

---

[1] We choose to use *Yu* instead of more common *You* as our translation of the Chinese character 有. This is for its symmetry with *Wu*. The correct ancient pronunciation of this character is of course controversial.

After extensive comparative studies with other ancient East and West philosophies, our thoughts become mature and we can present the principle with clarity. The process to arrive at our current conclusion is strenuous and is not possible to describe here. In essence, it is a long iteration of our interpretations of the *Tao Te Ching* and an emerging principle. The iterations converge slowly to show the emerging principle.

The final breakthroughs occur suddenly in the successful interpretation of the first chapter of the *Tao Te Ching*. This breakthrough allows us to extract a clear principle from this single Chapter! Most other Chapters may be treated as footnotes to this principle. The critical breakthrough is the meaning of the Chinese character Heng (恆) and the symmetry between Wu and Yu.

Of course, we may not think like our ancient philosophers in many ways; but our ability to recognize the *core principle* of nature should be unchanged. We should be able to recognize the same principle in our current reading of the *Tao Te Ching*. As Lao-tzu says in Chapter 14: we can see the way of the ancient Tao in our affairs of today. [1]

---

[1] As said in Chapter 14: Following the Tao of today, we can manage the affairs of today, as the way to know about its ancient beginning.

Fortunately, our journey ends with a clear logical structure of Tao philosophy and we can formulate an intuitively scientific model to show this logical structure and the principle behind this structure. This model may be validated with the first chapter of the *Tao Te Ching*. We can show the principle of Tao clearly and we can validate this model in a consistent interpretation of the whole *Tao Te Ching*.

The Principle of Tao Philosophy

After extensive analysis, we are surprised to find this principle embedded in the first chapter of the *Tao Te Ching*. It can be summarized as *The Principle of Oneness*. Tao philosophy is a philosophy of nature, and the whole nature may be represented as Oneness. Lao-tzu describes the way to maintain reality in our "dualistic thinking," with this principle. Therefore, Tao philosophy may be called the *Philosophy of Oneness* or a *Non-duality* philosophy.

From the Principle of Oneness, we can establish two other related principles: the Principle of Complementarity and the Principle of Equivalence. These will be discussed in detail in Chapter II.

Lao-tzu has summarized this principle in an extremely concise form. Later, we have also found the same principle in the Pre-Socratic philosophy, modern Western philosophy, and Eastern philosophies, such as Hinduism and Buddhism. Such comparative studies have greatly helped clarify the principle observed in the *Tao Te Ching*. Now we are convinced that the *Tao Te Ching* is logical and its principle is precise. We can be quite confident that Lao-tzu is an authentic philosopher.

A Language-independent Principle

There have been numerous translations and interpretations of the *Tao Te Ching*. Most scholars attribute our difficulties to the differences between the languages (ancient and modern, Chinese and others). As we have already pointed out in the *Dynamic Tao and Its Manifestations*, the fundamental difficulty is not the differences in languages but is due to a lack of understanding of the *principle* in the original language. Therefore, we are unable to translate or interpret properly.

There have been ample examples that we can successfully translate complicated principles in science and philosophy from one language to another. This is because if we have understood the principle, the translation of the principle will not be severely hampered by the differences in languages. Therefore, I believe that we have been hampered by the lack of a philosophical principle in the historical interpretations of the *Tao Te Ching*.

This lack of principle is introduced in its native Chinese language. Many interpretations do not have a consistent principle. Most Western scholars have simply carried over the difficulties embedded in the Chinese historical commentaries.

Now, this will completely change. With a clear principle, our interpretation will be language-independent. That is, if we understand the principle of Tao in one language, we will be able to formulate the same principle in any other language. The essence of all translations of the *Tao Te Ching* is to translate the principle; rhetoric renderings are secondary in the translation. All languages should be able to describe the basic principle of Tao.

Breaking-Out of an Endless Loop

Throughout the years, our understanding of Tao philosophy has been going around an endless circle without new insight. It is very common that, in most analyses of Tao, one starts without logic, analyzes the commentaries assuming no logic, and concludes that there is no logic in Tao.

Such a closed-loop analysis has perpetuated the myth that Tao philosophy does not have logic. Most scholars simply reiterate the historical contradictory Chinese commentaries. We need to break out of this closed loop.

We need a new start. Without a new approach, both the East and the West will continue to be hampered by the same difficulties. The mysteries of Tao will likely continue in a tight loop.

Our model will be a convenient platform to break out of such an endless loop. We shall arrive at the new horizon and see the logic of Tao philosophy with scientific clarity.

Think like a Chinese?

Without an apparent logic, the *Tao Te Ching* does not fit into the Western philosophical system. Faced with such difficulty, many thinkers have taken Tao as a unique kind of Chinese thinking. Some claim that Tao is far superior and cannot be analyzed in terms of Western or scientific ideas. A few even suggest that Western scholars should "think like a Chinese" to solve these issues that cannot be resolved by Chinese thinkers logically. Most Western philosophers follow Chinese thinking and simply accept Tao as a non-systematic philosophy.

This fact is reflected in the fact that, in the academic world, Tao philosophy and other Eastern philosophy are considered Asian Thoughts outside Philosophy Departments.

We should not think in the old Chinese way that alienates itself from logic and "scientific reasoning."

A Perennial Philosophy

The Perennial Philosophy views each of the world's philosophical traditions as sharing a single, universal logic model of knowledge and doctrine. The various principles in Tao philosophy are very fundamental and general in our basic search for reality. These principles may be called the *fundamental principle* of the Perennial Philosophy.

In a separate book, *Searching for the Meaning of Life*[1] we have surveyed this common logical principle in religions, psychology, and many philosophical discourses.

Lao-tzu proclaims his Principle

It is worth mentioning that during our early stage of research, we assume the principle of Tao is well hidden. The first sign of Lao-tzu as a philosopher came as a surprise in his proclamation that there is a *principle* in his teachings. He proclaims that "All teachings have their principles and all efforts have their guiding rules."[2]

---

[1] Wang, Wayne L., *Searching for the Meaning of Life*, Helena Island Publisher, 2014.

[2] Chapter 70: 言有宗，事有君。

This proclamation has not been widely recognized. After more than 10 years of research, we finally come to a grip of this principle and rediscover this principle in the *Tao Te Ching*. I can conclude that the *Tao Te Ching* is a genuine philosophical text and Lao-tzu has a principle.

The principle is clear and we have to avoid finding justifications for any inconsistent views encountered about Tao. For example, we do not need to associate the meanings of the *Tao Te Ching* with the turmoil of the Warring States (403 – 221 BCE)[1] and we do not take the words of Lao-tzu as anti-Confucian rhetoric. The principle of Tao is more fundamental than a view on historical and social situations.

Refocusing the Mysteries of Tao

The mysteries of Tao do not disappear because we have found its principle. We have to refocus on the mysteries. The core mystery of Tao is in the principle of Tao itself. With our models, this principle can be comprehended, we still face the formidable challenge of presenting this principle to the public since our enthusiasm about Tao is mostly powered by the historical paradoxes and mysteries.

---

[1] It is very common that the "paradoxical" thoughts of Lao-tzu are taken to be the results of the turmoil in the Lao-tzu's era. On the contrary, we seldom attribute the thoughts of the Presocratics or Socrates to the wars and turmoil of their era.

We have reduced these paradoxes and mysteries of Tao into a few principles. These principles are common in many other philosophies and modern sciences. We have to abandon the historical mysteries of Tao and accept the new paradigm.

This will be a great change in our thinking habits about Tao. We have to leap into a new paradigm. To guide our minds systematically and logically, we shall choose scientific models to steer our minds away from our habitual thinking and historical speculations. This systematic model is a convenient way to avoid falling again into the traditional paradoxes and contradictions.

A Systematic Model

Many of our conclusions are opposite to the prevailing and powerful views on Tao philosophy. For this reason, we have to articulate our approach carefully and clearly. For an accurate formulation that can be analyzed systematically, we borrow two popular "scientific" methods.

These methods may already be familiar to many readers due to the popularization of sciences, but some readers may have to overcome the uneasiness of physics and mathematics.

This model is common in many other philosophical and scientific discussions. Our basic thinking patterns in science and philosophy are compatible. The common feature is the Oneness of nature. Science and philosophy are different observations of the same principle of nature.

This common principle is called the first principle in philosophy. In sciences, it is also the foundation of many theories. Therefore, we can approach this philosophy with scientific formulations. What is in common is their basic logical thinking.

Neither do we claim the specific mysteries of Tao are scientific phenomena, nor do we believe that there is definite scientific foresight in Lao-tzu's Tao philosophy.

Structure of this Book

We divide this book into two parts with a total of six Chapters.

Part I is a complete description of the logic of Tao philosophy. In this Part, we have three Chapters. Chapter I is a short Introduction of our journey in the search for this principle of Tao. Chapter II discusses the Principle of Tao in terms of the first chapter of the *Tao Te Ching*. This Chapter is all background for our model. Chapter III presents the formal model in detail. This model deals with the nature of dualistic thinking and our linguistic description of reality. This part identifies the logic of Tao philosophy.

Part II describes the applications of this logic model and principles in the interpretation of the *Tao Te Ching*. The Part also has three Chapters. Chapter IV reviews the characteristics of the model. Chapter V comments on the several common errors in the historical interpretations. It also reviews new interpretations of the key concepts. Chapter VI is a summary.

Appendix A applies the same model to the trichotomy of time. Appendix B lists the main keywords.

A new Translation and a Graphic Novel

We publish a new translation of the *Tao Te Ching* based on this model: *The Tao Te Ching: an Ultimate Translation*. We are also preparing a Graphic Novel to interpret the *Tao Te Ching* less formally. These books are in our *Searching for Tao Series*.

Chapter II
The Principle of Tao

We make up our minds to name two modes of manifestation for a reality ... We must not discuss the two modes as two separate and independent realities; otherwise, we will go astray.

Parmenides

Original reality is one, but is manifested as function (phenomenon); hence, it has to be differentiated. If we say that there are different parts, we are talking with respect to the appearances of function. Although the appearances of function are differentiated into various parts, these parts are not different with respect to the original reality.

Xiong Shili 熊十力

In this Chapter, we shall show that Tao philosophy has a well-defined principle and Lao-tzu has described it very well in the first chapter of the *Tao Te Ching*. This principle of Tao has never been identified since it is encoded with extreme skill and precision. It has defied logical decoding for the last 2000 years.

We shall discuss the logical structure of Tao and identify the principles of Tao and use these as a foundation for developing the formal scientific model in Chapter III.

Like most others, I have fallen under the overwhelming mystery of Tao in the beginning. The logic structure and the principles appear only after extraneous efforts. The mystery of Tao suddenly disappears after we find the principle in the first chapter of the Tao Te Ching. The clarity of Lao-tzu's description is well beyond our imagination and is far more accurate than other philosophical descriptions of the same principle.

We may now reveal the principle of Tao from within the first chapter of the Tao Te Ching. The once-formidable chapter can now be interpreted naturally and clearly without much speculation.

Our result might appear as a shock to many readers and scholars, even though many scholars have recognized the importance of the first chapter of the *Tao Te Ching*. For example, the notable Professor Wing-tsit Chan (1963) describes the chapter as "the most important of all chapters" that shows the basic characteristics of Tao. He says, "This chapter both introduces and summarizes the entire *Tao Te Ching*. The 'five thousand' words of the text are all based on this chapter." However, these observations have not been elaborated with analysis.

This book claims a historical "breakthrough" in decoding the first chapter of the *Tao Te Ching*, and the "discovery" of the principle of Tao philosophy. Throughout history, there have been many similar claims. However, most of the claims are short-lived. Ambiguities and paradoxes return again and again. We are confident in our findings and shall make our claim accessible to open scrutiny.

Historically, there have been some textual variations in the first chapter of the *Tao Te Ching*. For our purpose, such variations do not alter our conclusion. To show clearly the keywords and the logic structure, we adopt a combined Mawangdui 馬王堆 and Wang Bi 王弼 texts. The most critical characteristics are the keyword Heng 恆 and the symmetry of Wu and Yu.[1]

Our textual parsing of the first Chapter is unique. I preserve the meaning of Heng 恆 and the symmetry of Wu 無 and Yu 有 in the first Chapter. With this, the first Chapter may be parsed into five verses:

---

[1] We choose Mawangdui version of Verse 2 and its explicit use of Heng. In Verse 2, Wang Bi has "Wu names the origin of "heaven and earth." The Mawangdui text uses both Wu and Yu to refer to the myriad things. In many cases, "heaven and earth" and the "myriad things" are synonyms, but sometimes, Tao itself is the root of "heaven and earth" [Ch.6] Later, Wang Bi takes Wu to be Tao and thus violate the logic structure discussed in the book.

Chapter II The Principle of Tao

1 Tao may be spoken of, but it is not the Heng Tao;
   Names may be named, but it is not the Heng Name.
2 Wu names the origin of the myriad things;
   Yu names the mother of the myriad things.
3 However,
   In Heng Wu, we observe their mysterious appearances;
   In Heng Yu, we observe their fading boundaries.
4 Both appear simultaneously, as
   different manifestations of the same (Tao).
5 Obscurity upon obscurity,
   They are the gateways to all mysteries.

Let us follow the above scenario of Lao-tzu carefully. In the above parsing, we recognize the special meaning of Heng and the complete symmetry in the pairs of "Tao-Name," "Wu-Yu," and "Heng Wu-Heng Yu." Such parsing allows us to see the structure of the Chapter that can be analyzed systematically.

The special meaning of Heng is "holistic," and therefore realistic and persistent. Heng is beyond and before any dualistic division. "Heng" associates a name (as a Heng name, Heng Tao, Heng Wu, and Heng Yu) with reality or with wholeness.

In this Chapter, Wu and Yu may be any two opposite concepts. This is a common dualism. The discussion of Lao-tzu is about how to preserve reality in a dualism.

Since parsing of the text in the first Chapter is critical, we show Chinese text for reference.

1 　道、可道也，非恆道也；
　　名、可名也，非恆名也。
2 　無、名萬物之始；
　　有、名萬物之母。
3 　故
　　恆無、欲以觀其所妙；
　　恆有、欲以觀其所徼。
4 　兩者同出，異名同謂。
5 　玄之又玄，眾妙之門。

Brief Summary of the First Chapter

In the first Chapter, the reality is Tao. Tao is the proper relations of the myriad things in the phenomenal world, where we assign various names to the myriad things. Tao has no name in the phenomenal world, so it remains nameless.

Heng Tao 恆道 and Heng Name 恆名 are the true reality of Tao and the true relations between the myriad things. We are used to describing the relations with simple dualistic concepts. Lao-tzu introduces two well-defined Wu 無 and Yu 有 to describe the relations of the myriad things, but the true relations are Heng Wu 恆無 and Heng Yu 恆有.

We call Wu and Yu the objects, and Heng Wu and Heng Yu the actualities. The logic of Tao philosophy is the way the objects can be used to describe the actualities.

The first Verse is a simple opening statement that expresses the limitation of our language. Verse 2 defines two *objects*, Wu and Yu, to describe the myriad things. Wu means "without differentiation." Yu means "with differentiation." [1]

Lao-tzu uses Verse 3 to introduce two *true manifestations* of Tao as Heng Wu 恆無 and Heng Yu 恆有 as the true relationships between the myriad things. Lao-tzu's description is very skillful.

---

[1] If we parse this verse as "Without Name" and "With Name," "Without Name" may refer to Tao and "With Name" refer to the phenomenal world. But such parsing cannot concisely reveal the logic of the whole chapter.

In the undifferentiated Heng Wu, we see the appearances of differences (Yu). In the differentiated Heng Yu, we see fading boundaries of the differences (Wu)." Lao-tzu soon discovers that each true manifestation is a complementarity of both Wu and Yu.

In Verse 4, Lao-tzu further states that the two actualities are simultaneous and equivalent manifestations of the same Tao. This is a very important feature in the logic of Tao philosophy.

Finally, in Verse 5, Lao-tzu characterizes the two manifestations as *obscure upon obscure* 玄之又玄. Obscurity means that the manifestation cannot be clearly described as Wu or Yu. All linguistic descriptions of the manifestations are "vague and indeterminate." This is the definition of Obscurity. All mysteries of Tao are in the obscurity of these manifestations. Once we understand the nature of this obscurity, we can apprehend the core mystery of Tao.

Basic Concept of Heng

Heng is the central theme in the first Chapter. Our textual arrangement is based on the recognition of the word *Heng* 恆 as the central concept of Tao. We cannot describe or translate Heng in a simple way, so I leave it untranslated. In the logic of Tao philosophy, Heng has a definite meaning.

Chapter II The Principle of Tao

The word Heng in the first Chapter was discovered only in 1993, so it has not been properly recognized in the traditional interpretations.[1] My realization of the importance of this recognition was inspired by Professor Qingjie Wang [Wang 2000]. Because of the special meaning of this word, the structure of the first Chapter can be completely revealed.

Heng preserves the nature of wholeness and its property is equivalent to Oneness. All philosophies emphasize that reality must have wholeness. This is also the key concept in Tao philosophy. This is our *Principle of Oneness*.

In ordinary language, we have lost most words that can preserve wholeness. Heng comprises of both "changing and unchanging," or "eternal and non-eternal," etc. Heng is similar to Change (易) in the Book of Change (易經) but has encountered similar difficulties. Change comprises of "Change" and "Un-change." Heng is also the core of the Book of Change.

The objects are fragmented; Heng Wu and Heng Yu preserve wholeness. The logic of Tao philosophy is to preserve wholeness in the description of reality.

---

[1] The word Heng 恆 was replaced by Chang 常 after Liu Heng 劉恆 became the emperor of Han dynasty (180-157 BCE). Heng reappeared in the Mawangdui version unearthed in 1973.

Analysis of the First Chapter

Tao represents the order of the myriad things. We distinguish the myriad things according to this order. The myriad things include all thoughts; therefore, Tao is the proper order of our thoughts. Our thinking must obey this order to be realistic. We cannot describe this order directly, but we can search for this order in the proper relations of the myriad things.

Lao-tzu describes clearly this order in the first chapter of the *Tao Te Ching*. It may surprise many that this principle of Tao is presented clearly and precisely in the Chapter because this Chapter has long been considered very fuzzy and hard to decode.

1. Heng Tao and Heng Name

As an opening statement of the *Tao Te Ching*, Lao-tzu simply acknowledges the limitations of our language. This is a simple fact. It is very difficult to describe reality in language. Such limitation of language is well recognized in both East and West philosophy.

"Tao can be talked about" and "names can be named" affirm that we can use language to describe Tao. Heng Tao is the principle of nature. In the phenomenal world, all linguistic descriptions of the myriad things must obey this principle, so the description is the realistic Heng Names.

2. Wu and Yu as Conventional Objects

In Verse 2, Lao-tzu uses Wu and Yu as the conventional dualistic description of the nature of the myriad things. Such simple dualism considers Wu and Yu as two mutually exclusive concepts. Lao-tzu associates Wu and Yu with two fundamental characteristics of the myriad things. He defines Wu and Yu as: [1]

- Wu indicates that, in the beginning, the myriad things are undifferentiated. Before they are formed, the myriad things are indistinguishable from one another.
- Yu indicates that when the myriad things are formed, the myriad things are fully distinguishable. Each thing has a clear boundary from the other.

Therefore, Wu and Yu are well-defined, distinctively different, and mutually exclusive, concepts. In such a dualistic framework, the myriad things are either all the same or all different. [2] However, the "true" characteristics of the myriad things cannot be either Wu or Yu.

---

[1] In the Mawangdui version, both Wu and Yu are associated with the myriad things. This shows the scope of Tao as the philosophy of nature. In Wang Bi's version, Wu is defined as the "origin of Heaven and Earth" instead of the "origin of the myriad things."

[2] Wu and Yu describe "sameness" and the "difference" of the myriad things.

Nevertheless, we can still use Wu and Yu as the common language to describe the true characteristics of the myriad things. These objects are the traditional discussion of Sameness and Difference.

3. Heng Wu and Heng Yu as Realities

In Verse 3, Lao-tzu introduces Heng Wu and Heng Yu to describe the *true* characteristics of the myriad things. The true characteristics must cover the whole domain of Tao, so they must re-integrate the two sub-domains of Wu and Yu into a whole.

Lao-tzu has a skillful method to describe Heng Wu and Heng Yu. This is the real order of nature and the real order of the myriad things. Lao-tzu's description is quite natural:

- In the state of Heng Wu, we also see the boundary of the myriad things appearing. Lao-tzu uses "subtlety 妙" to indicate "subtle appearances of the myriad things." Wu with the complementarity of Yu forms Heng Wu.
- In the state of Heng Yu, we also see the boundaries of the myriad things disappearing. Lao-tzu uses "borderless 徼" to indicate the "disappearance of the boundaries between the myriad things." Yu with the complementarity of Yu forms Heng Yu.

In Lao-tzu's description, Wu and Yu *complement* each other to form Heng Wu and Heng Yu. Thus, Heng Wu and Heng Yu overcome the fragmentation of Wu and Yu and preserve the wholeness of Tao. This is the *Principle of Complementarity* in Tao.

4. Same Time and the Same Tao

In Verse 4, Lao-tzu emphasizes that these two manifestations "appear at the same time" and "describe the same reality with different names." This is a critical statement in the logic of Tao philosophy.

The two manifestations do not have cyclic appearances. They represent the same principle of Tao. Therefore, the two manifestations are *ontologically equivalent*.[1] This is our *Principle of Equivalence*.

---

[1] Professor Lik-kuen Tong uses the term "Ontological Equivalence" in his description of Tao philosophy. (Tong 2001) Such relation appears in the Western philosophy with various names, e.g., the *Principle of Ontological Parity* of Rene Guenon.

5. Mysteries of Tao as Profound

In the last Verse, Lao-tzu characterizes the manifestations of Tao as "obscurity upon obscurity." These manifestations are obscure because we cannot describe them as clearly as Wu and Yu. Wu and Yu are always superimposed and complementary within the manifestation. Linguistic descriptions of manifestations will always appear fuzzy, indeterminate, and self-contradictory. That is the obscurity of Tao.

The Basic Architecture

According to the above interpretation, the first Chapter is a precise summary of the principle of Tao philosophy. We may construct a complete logic structure of Tao philosophy according to this Chapter. To make our discussion clear, we may use Figure 1 to show the basic logic structure of Tao philosophy.

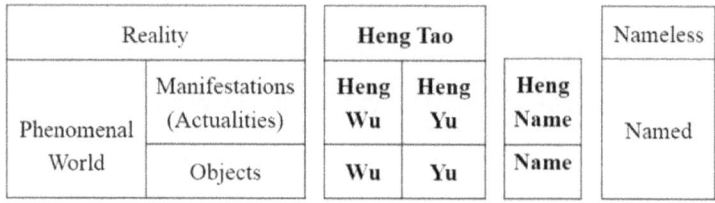

Figure 1 Basic Architecture of Tao Philosophy

In Figure 1, the bold-faced terms are the keywords used by Lao-tzu in the first Chapter. In this basic structure, our discussion starts with the dualistic concepts of Wu and Yu as our common language. Heng Wu and Heng Yu are complex of Wu and Yu. In

Here, Heng Tao represents the *absolute reality*, which is reflected as the ultimate nature of the myriad things in the phenomenal world. The myriad things are designated with two levels: Names and Heng Names, corresponding to the Object and Actuality levels.

In a metaphysical framework, the actualities are manifestations of Tao. In the phenomenal world, Tao itself has no manifestation, so it has "no name." The manifestations of Tao and the actualities of the objects are synonyms.

The three levels in this basic architecture have the same level of reality. Each level must preserve the same reality. In other words, the same principle of Tao must be observed at each level in our formulation.

Actualities and Manifestations

In model discussion, we shall use actuality and manifestations interchangeably. In general discussions, the Heng Wu and Heng Yu are called the actualities. In Tao philosophy, these actualities may also be called the Heng-Actualities (恆象), according to the definition of Heng.

We may look at Fig.1 in two ways. From the object level, Wu and Yu integrate into Heng Wu and Heng Yu. This is induction. We may also see Heng Wu and Heng Yu as the manifestations of Tao, which are then resulted in objects. This is reduction. These two processes of thinking are equivalent and supplementary.

We designate three levels to discuss the same reality, so each level must have the same reality and reflect the same principle of Tao. Such structure is similar to the traditional phenomenology, but Lao-tzu does not discuss how actualities are formed from reality. He only describes how to preserve reality in dualistic thinking.

We have to find a logical combination of objects to describe reality. Lao-tzu does not deny the reality of objects and actualities. Although the reality of the objects is limited, a combination of language may describe the actualities according to the principle of Tao.

The absolute reality gives us a principle. All our discussions are in the phenomenal world. We have to distinguish two kinds of names in the phenomenal world:

- At the object level, each object has a distinct name and represents a "part" of the whole. The objects must be interconnected to preserve the whole. The reality at the object level must consist of the objects and their interconnections.
- At the actuality level, each actuality has a Heng name and is holistic. All actualities have equivalent reality. Each actuality represents the same reality in different ways.

The objects must be correlated logically to form actualities, so each actuality is a complex of objects. The logical correlation is in the form of *Complementarity*. The two objects will form two actualities that represent the same reality, so the two actualities are *ontologically equivalent*.

In this structure, the absolute reality and the two manifestations form a logical structure of the Trinity. The two ontologically equivalent actualities form a *Doctrine of Two Truths*. The object level and the actuality level also form a Doctrine of Two Truths.

The Principles of Tao Philosophy

We have analyzed the structure of the first chapter of the *Tao Te Ching* and identified the principle of Tao philosophy. This principle appears throughout the Tao Te Ching. We may express this principle as the Principle of Oneness, the Principle of Complementarity, and the Principle of Equivalence.

The Principle of Oneness

In dualism. Two simple opposite concepts are not sufficient to describe reality. The absolute reality is Oneness and each actuality must have a wholeness to describe the reality.

The two actualities may have different characteristics; however, they are two equivalent representations of the same reality. Wholeness in the phenomenal world must preserve the Oneness of Tao. The two actualities are equivalent and appear at the same time, so the reality has not been divided. This is the Principle of Oneness.

Each actuality contains opposite concepts and, therefore, will have interferences. When rendered into language, the actuality will appear as fuzzy and indeterminate, as obscurity. However, such fuzzy and indeterminate language is the proper way to understand accurately the nature of reality.

The Principle of Oneness is also the core of early Greek philosophy, Indian philosophy, and Buddhist philosophy. The Principle is also observed by most modern philosophers and scientific investigations.

The Principle of Complementarity

Two opposite objects complement each other to form the actualities. Therefore, the realistic representations for a reality always consist of two opposite objects in the pattern of complementarity. An individual object has no reality. This is the Principle of Complementarity.

Complementarity is a complex concept to understand. Fortunately, such a complementarity phenomenon is well-known in quantum theory where two objective views of particle and wave are reconciled. Complementarity is not a quantum concept. For example, when a piece of iron is magnetized, we may use "negative and positive" poles to describe the magnet, but these two poles cannot exist by themselves. The real negative pole is connected to the positive pole; the real positive pole is connected to the negative pole.

Lao-tzu does not deny the usefulness of our conventional knowledge as objects. However, he constantly reminds us that we should not take any object to be a reality. If we take these objects as realities, then we fall into the reductionism fallacy and distort the logical structure of reality.

The Principle of Equivalence

At the object level, the objects are mutually exclusive. However, at the actuality level, the two objects form complementary patterns as two actualities. These actualities are not mutually exclusive, but exist at the same time and are equivalent. This is the Principle of equivalence" in Tao.

This may seem illogical in the formal logic system. It is logical at the actual level because the actuality is a complementarity of two opposite objects. As discussed by Glen, the two actualities can only be of "Subcontrary Opposites," so they may both be true. His simple example is the equivalence between "Some men are musical" and "Some men are not musical."[1]

Another popular example is the equivalence between "The cup is half-full" and "The cup is half empty." "Full" and "Empty" are two opposites, but when we take "A Cup" as a whole, then the two statements are equivalent.

We may state this principle paradoxically as: "The opposite of a Truth is another Truth." This Truth is Ontological Truth at the actuality level. The truth at the object level is the Logical Truth.

This principle applies in any dualistic view. For example, the actuality level and the object level are also equivalent to reflecting reality.

---

[1] Glen (1947), p.179.

A Systematic Model

This Chapter covers the principle of Tao philosophy. However, such textual description is often ambiguous. Therefore, we shall develop a more rigorous model in the next Chapter to show the logical relationship of the various concepts.

The purpose of this model is to guide our thinking systematically, to recognize the principle of Tao. Such a novel approach is necessary because our traditional thinking often falls back into historical errors.

In this model discussion, Lao-tzu's logic is rather precise and systematic, as he describes in the first chapter of the *Tao Te Ching*. This system can be seen in the first chapter of the Tao Te Ching, without much speculation. Its principles are repeatedly reflected in the Chapters of the Tao Te Ching. Once we understand this model, we will be able to comprehend the meaning of the *Tao Te Ching* directly in the words of Lao-tzu. The model is only a step-stone, the principle of Tao will become self-evident.

Thus, we can overcome our confusion in historical interpretations and correct some popular misinterpretations. Although our immediate purpose is to understand and analyze Tao philosophy, our model is a general philosophical logic model. We may also see the proper role Tao philosophy plays in world philosophy.

PART II
CHARACTERISTICS OF THE MODEL
AND
NEW INTERPRETATIONS

Chapter III
The Logic of Tao Philosophy

> *Looked at from anywhere, the world is full of insecurities and contradictions; looked at from Nowhere, it is a changeless, uniform whole."*
>
> Arthur Waley
> The Way and Its Power

> *Proceed thus: if you say "The Good, add nothing in your thought: for if you add something, you will diminish it by as much as you add."*
>
> Plotinus (204 -270 CE)

In this chapter, we shall discuss a systematic model of the logic of Tao philosophy. We use two basic "scientific" models to delineate the logic of Tao philosophy. These models will be very helpful for those who are versed in the sciences so they can make connections to scientific interpretations. However, we shall provide detailed textual explanations of the principle for those not familiar with scientific models.

We shall show how Lao-tzu uses his linguistic logic to describe the principle of Tao. The logic model has two parts. The first part is an *Interaction Model* that describes how the two objects interact to form two actualities. The second part is a *Linguistic Model* which shows how we reduce concepts to language.

This logic model describes the proper relations between the myriad things in the phenomenal world. The myriad things include all conceptual objects. We are accustomed to thinking in terms of opposite objects, but actualities cannot be expressed with simple dualistic concepts and must be logical combinations of the objects. Objects will produce holistic actualities, but they do not exist within actualities. The interconnection between the objects is represented as their interactions in the model. We have two equivalent actualities. This is different from Hegel's logic.

In Lao-tzu's example, the objects are Wu and Yu. The objects could be any pair of opposite entities. This model is applicable in the discussion of any dualistic thinking.

The Logic of Tao Philosophy

To discuss reality with language has two distinct steps. First, we have to construct realistic concepts in our conventional dualistic thinking. Second, we have to express these realistic concepts in language. This Chapter will use a complete model to delineate the realistic concepts and their expression in language.

The first chapter of the *Tao Te Ching* uses dualistic thinking to show how we can establish realistic dualistic concepts. We have:

- Wu and Yu are two opposite objects that can be directly expressed in language;
- Heng Wu and Heng Yu are two realistic complex concepts that can be expressed in terms of the objects.

In this step, we use Wu and Yu to construct Heng Wu and Heng Yu. We identify objects as simple *objective* concepts that can be expressed in definite language. Actualities are complex concepts that are formed with a certain structure of objects. We need an *Interaction Model* to show the formation of actuality and its structure.

An actuality is a complex of two interfering concepts that will interfere with each other. Such interference makes linguistic expression complicated. Therefore, we need a Linguistic Model to show the result of such interferences.

The Model Architecture

We may show the basic architecture of this model in Fig. 2. The objects, Wu and Yu, are simple concepts to describe Heng Tao. These objects interact and intermix to form Heng Wu and Heng Yu, as the actualities.

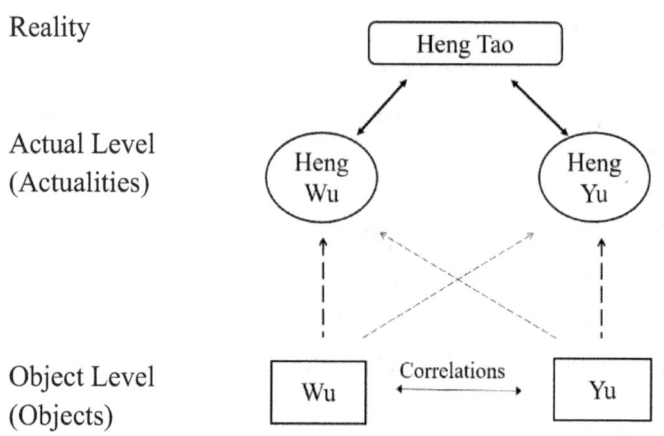

Figure 2 Interaction Model Architecture

The interactions hold two parts Wu and Yu together as a whole to preserve the reality at the Object Level. The actualities are free of any interaction.

Actualization and Objectification

Fig.2 may be viewed in two different directions. In the first chapter of the *Tao Te Ching,* Lao-tzu defines the objects first, and then the objects are used to describe the actualities. The upward process is called *Actualization*. In the downward process, we comprehend the appearance of the actualities and identify the objects to describe these actualities. The downward process is called *Objectification.* Objectification *collapses* a whole actuality into an object or object.

Actualization and articulation occur at the same time and are reversible. In either way, they are bound by the same principle. In the phenomenal world, the two levels "appear at the same time and represent the same reality with different patterns." We often think in terms of the Object Level.

Interactions between Objects

Although Lao-tzu never explicitly mentions the interactions between Wu and Yu, we know that reality cannot be separated into two separate objects. We have to introduce interactions to avoid the fragmentation of reality. Such interactions must follow certain principles to reconstruct realistic actualities.

The interactions ensure that the objects will participate to form a particular relation within the actualities. Each actuality will have different relation consisting of the objects. However, these two actualities are equivalent since they are formed by the same interaction between the same objects.

The only condition for this interaction is that the actuality must be free from any interaction and independent. This is a very special condition. Therefore, the interactions between the objects must produce stable actualities. This is the only condition that we can use to solve this model. We do not have to know the nature of this interaction to have a clear result of the interaction.

We shall note that the interactions "exist" only at the object level. Whenever we think in terms of the objects, there will be interactions. The only purpose of these interactions is to drive all objects to form actualities that can represent reality. Such interactions are teleological.

The Complete Logic Model

Logic is to use language to describe reality. Language represents our mature simple concepts. Reality is in general a complex of concepts that cannot be easily rendered in language.

To develop a complete logic model, we have to take two distinct steps. Firstly, we need to identify the *conceptual relationship* between actualities and objects. Secondly, we need to express these concepts in our ordinary language. Therefore, we have two sub-models:

- An Interaction Model to establish the *conceptual relationship* between actualities and objects;
- A Linguistic Model to render concepts to language.

These two sub-models constitute a complete logic model. We shall try to keep the *scientific* formulation to a minimum. Nevertheless, we have decided to keep a few mathematical and graphic descriptions in the discussion, because such analytic forms do provide additional benefits for our understanding of the intricate logic structure of Tao philosophy.

The Interaction Model

This Interaction Model will provide a conceptual relationship between objects and actualities. The objects are our conventional starting points for our communication.

Lao-tzu first defines Wu and Yu as two opposite objects to characterize the nature of the myriad things. However, such characterization is too simplistic. The myriad things cannot be Wu nor Yu. Therefore, he points out the true nature of the myriad things as Heng Wu and Heng Yu, each with an intermixture of Wu and Yu. Our task is then to find a logical way to form the actualities from these interacting objects.

The actuality must be whole, independent, and self-sustaining. Therefore, there is no interaction between the actualities. The Interaction Model may be shown in Fig. 3.

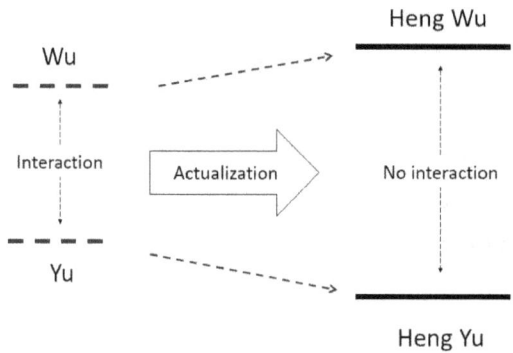

Figure 3 The Actualization Process

In this process, the objects and the actualities are treated as *conceptual states*, so they can be mixed and superimposed. The objects are unstable due to their interactions, and they form stable actualities because of their interactions. Fig.3. shows the actualization process.

Such an interaction model is commonly used in sciences to find stable states from unstable states. In science, we often assume the interactions to determine the proper final states. However, in our interaction model, we do not know the interactions, but we know the actualities must be stable. This is a critical observation in this model. Without this condition, we could not solve the problem.

Relational Structure of Actualities

In science, the result of such actualization is well-known. We shall show the analytic solution without mathematical derivations. The final conceptual states <Heng Wu> and <Heng Yu> may be expressed in the following equations as (The states are represented as <x >.):

$$< \text{Heng Wu} > \ = \ a < \text{Wu} > \ + \ b < \text{Yu} >$$
$$< \text{Heng Yu} > \ = \ a < \text{Yu} > \ - \ b < \text{Wu} >$$

Equation 1 Relational Structure of Actualities

The actuality is a *superposition* of the objects. We shall see that actuality is formed by *fusion,* not a mixture, of the opposite objects. The superposition of opposite concepts will display interesting *interference* characteristics. This will be discussed in our Linguistic Model.

The Principle of Complementarity

These mathematical relationships show the internal structure of the actualities in terms of the objects. The two objects proportionally (with a, b) participate in the formation of the actualities.

We may identify such a relationship as *complementarity* of Wu and Yu. The coefficients (a, b) represent the degree of participation of each object in the actualities; their values are determined by the strength of the interactions.

If the objects chosen are already close to the actualities, the interaction will be weak and the mixing will be small (b << a); if the objects chosen are far from the actualities, the interaction will be strong, and the mixing will be large ($a \approx b$). This equation also shows how the two parts can be recombined into a whole.

The two actualities are internally coupled through (a, b), so they are not truly independent. The structure of the actuality is determined by the principle of interactions in Tao. The structure ensures that the objects are completely harmonized within the actuality. This is the *Principle of Complementarity*.

Reality is Indivisible

The two actualities have different characteristics, but both are results of the same interaction and same pair of objects. Although reality has two actualities, the two actualities are equivalent representations of the same reality. They still cover the same wholeness of the domain. Therefore, the reality is not divided into two. The actualities are multiple states of the same *Being*.

In many traditional discussions, a being cannot be divided and cannot have plurality or multiplicity. Here we have a new understanding that multiple actualities do not constitute a division of a being.

In *Tao Te Ching*, Lao-tzu uses many examples to explain the principle of complementarity. Only the complementarity of the opposites may have reality. For example, Chapter 28 has male-female, honor-disgrace, and black-white; Chapter 23 has division-whole, injustice-justice, shallow-full, exhaustion-renewal, scarcity-addition, abundance-reduction, etc. Although the opposite objects in the examples are different, their complementarity condition reflects the same principle of Tao.

Reality as Relational Proposition

Equation (1) shows that reality is a complementary relation of two opposite objects. That is, reality can be described only as a "relational proposition," and not an object. An object is only a part, not a whole.

In its simplest form, an actuality is always an internal harmonization of opposite objects. The objects are thoroughly entangled, mingled, blended, or fused. Such correlation is not the external balance between two objects, nor the cyclic appearance of two objects. Actuality is a holistic manifestation of complementarity from within.

We cannot describe any actuality without mentioning both objects. For this reason, if we think in terms of dualistic objects, the reality will be indefinite because of interferences. However, if we can overcome the interference between the objects, the reality is always clear and definite.[1]

Actualities reflect the same Principle

The relationship between the objects in the two actualities follows the same law of interactions and reflects the characteristics of the same reality. As long as we follow the principle of Tao, we can switch from one actuality to the other without any external effort. Therefore, there will be no deviation from reality in switching between the manifestations/actualities.

As mentioned before, there is no possibility of a cyclic transition between the objects or between actualities. The structure in the formulation is timeless, so any transition is an illusion. All objects and actualities exist at the same time. Due to our habit of thinking in terms of one object at a time, we often miscomprehend that objects and actualities can transition.

The two actualities are equivalent representations of the same reality. This is the *Principle of Equivalence* in Tao philosophy.

---

[1] We often think that a reality is limitless or infinite. It fact, a reality is only indefinite because we think in terms of dualistic objects.

Interference of superimposed Objects

S*uperimposed* of two objects will create *interferences*. Such interferences will create completely different characteristics in the actualities, showing the complementarity of objects. Interference is necessary to preserve the wholeness of reality.

Unless we can overcome the habit of thinking in terms of objects, superposition or the interferences of objects is very difficult to clarify. Logic is based on language, so it becomes very complicated because of these interferences. However, such interference is very common in physics and mathematics.

The only complementarity of objects can reveal the characteristics of actuality. When we think in terms of two objects, we are still thinking in a dualistic mode. The two opposite objects do not balance against each other. Complementarity is the internal balance of two objects from within a whole.[1] Since language is based on dualistic objects, such superposition is very difficult to describe with language. The linguistic expression will show self-contradiction. Such paradoxes appear, for example, in [Ch.36] as

---

[1] The complementarity is an *internal balance* of two objects from within. Our objects are *concepts* that can be intermixed within an actuality.

For it to shrink, it must have been already expanded.
For it to weaken, it must have been already strengthened.

The opposite pairs, (shrink, expand) and (weaken, strengthen), must be in the same statement to express a reality. Such statements are not self-contradictory but are complementary.

Fortunately, superposition is a common phenomenon in Physics and Mathematics, and we can use the same methodology to discuss conceptual interferences in the *Linguistic Model*.

Many-to-Many Relationship

The relation between the actualities and the objects is many-to-many. However, the actualities are not many since all actualities are equivalent; objects are not many since they are interrelated as a whole. When an object changes, all objects will also change and the structure of the actuality will change. However, it will maintain its wholeness.

When a new reality appears, we may select a new group of objects to cover the whole domain of reality and form a group of actualities to represent reality.

We should note that an object cannot become an actuality by itself, e.g., Wu cannot become Heng Wu by itself. Only dual objects can harmonize each other to produce dual "opposite, but equivalent" actualities.

The actualization process is not to combine two opposite objects into one actuality or another object. This is unlike the process of Hegel that could lead to a totalitarian system of thought. The logic of Tao philosophy always maintains plural representations for a reality.

Complementarity is not Self-Contradiction

Complementarity of the two objects within an actuality is not a "self-contradiction," since the objects have lost their inherent properties due to complementarity. Self-contradiction occurs only when we mistake two objects to be real. In other words, when we think in terms of objects, there will be self-contradictory in our thought of actuality. However, in actuality, the opposite objects are always complementary and in harmony, and the superficial contradiction will disappear to show the characteristics of reality.

We have to convince ourselves to accept the concept of complementarity. In Tao philosophy, a complementarity is a simple act of "mutual completion with the opposites (相反相成)." Complementarity appears very often in the *Tao Te Ching*, such as "division with wholeness 曲則全," "Great Square has no corner 大方無隅", or "great accomplishment appears deficient 大器免成." These words point to the inherent harmony of nature and are not self-contradictory.

The opposite nature of the objects disappears on the whole. These will appear to be mysterious. As Heraclitus says in his fragment: "They do not understand how that which differs with itself is in agreement: harmony consists of opposing tension, like that of the bow and lyre."

The Principle of Interactions

We can easily identify the opposite objects, but we are always wondering how the objects should interact to maintain harmony. At the object level, we choose two divided objects, so we must have this interaction to preserve the wholeness at the level. The interaction is to compensate for our artificial segregation of a whole into parts.

Such interaction maintains the principle of Tao and allows all objects to be in harmony. This interaction is often reflected as the *Power of Tao* imposed on the objects. However, this interaction appears only when we think in terms of the dual objects. On the actual level, such interaction does not exist.

The interactions of the myriad things should obey the principle of Tao. We can identify this *principle of interactions* as the Te 德 in Tao philosophy.

Chapter III The Logic of Tao Philosophy

Te and Tao are equally important in this Book of Tao and Te: Tao is the order of nature, and Te is the principle of interaction for an object to maintain this order of Tao.[1] In actuality, this order is called "The obscure Te (玄德)."

The Tai-Ji Symbol

Equation (1) is a basic relationship in Tao philosophy. Our mathematical results may appear puzzling to some readers. This is the *Basic Theory of Tao Philosophy*. The meaning of these mathematical relations is well-known in Chinese philosophy. It is the familiar *Tai-ji Symbol* 太極圖, as shown in Fig.4.

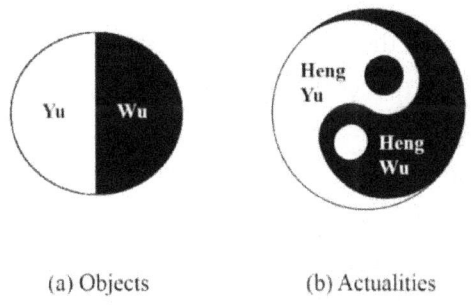

(a) Objects   (b) Actualities

Figure 4 The Tai-ji Symbol

---

[1] In Chuang-tzu *Heaven and Earth*: 故通於天者，道也；順於地者，德也；行於萬物者，義也。

Fig. 4 (a) is the traditional dualistic concept, where Wu and Yu are two completely segregated parts. Fig. 4(b) is the Tai-ji Symbol 太極圖, where Heng Wu and Heng Yu comprise of complementarity of Wu and Yu.

The familiar Tai-ji symbol shows the complementarity of Yin and Yang, but the meaning is the same for any opposite pair. In the Tai-ji symbol, the objects are not far from actualities, so each actuality consists of the main object and its complementary object. The two actualities are interconnected through the two "fish eyes," via the "dragon veins."

In Chapter 28, Lao-tzu identifies Tao as Wu-Ji 無極 (The Non-polarized polarized). The two manifestations of Tao are polarized to show the structure of Tai-ji. The structure of such polarization is the complementarity of the two objects. Therefore, our analytical model is fully consistent with the historical thought of Tai-ji. Such a relationship is a necessary result whenever we harmonize two opposite objects.

The term Tai-ji does not appear in the *Tao Te Ching*, but it appears in the *Yi-Chuang* 易傳, where we have "One Yin and One Yang is called Tao (一陰一陽之謂道)." The logical sequence is described as:

Wu-Ji gives birth to Tai-ji;
Tai-ji gives birth to two appearances;

The two actualities represent two universes that follow exactly the principle of Tao. The dragon vein acts as the "wormholes" to connect the two equivalent universes, thus having two parallel universes. Professor Niels Bohr, as the father of quantum physics, recognized the Tai-ji Symbol as similar to the complementarity in quantum theory and adopted it in his family "Coat of Arms."[1] Our understanding of complementarity in modern sciences can help us understand the complementarity in our thinking.

Reality Vectors and Coordinates

There are advantages to using an analytical model. The model is general and may have many equivalent interpretations. For example, we may discuss these mathematical relations in terms of a geometrical representation.

---

[1] Niels Bohr's coat of arms, designed in 1947. It was hung near the king's coat of arms in the church of Frederiksborg Castle at Hillerod. Bohr chose the yin-yang symbol. The Latin motto reads: "Opposites are complementary."

In such a representation, the domain of reality is thought space. The objects are the basis of our thinking that define the coordinates of this thought space. Then, the actualities are the reality vectors in this space. Geometrically, Eq.(1) may be shown in the following Figure.

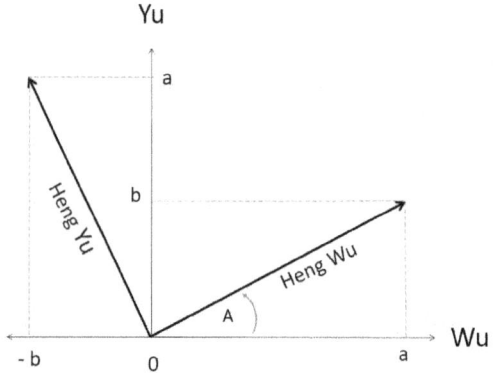

Figure 5 Thought Space and Reality Vectors

In this thought space, we think of Tao in terms of the objects <Wu> and <Yu>. The targets of our thought are the *reality vectors* (Heng Wu and Heng Yu). In general, our objects and the actualities do not coincide. The difference between our thought basis and the actualities may be represented by the angle "A."

In our pursuit of reality, we start with objects of thought and move toward the reality vectors, hoping to reach the final goals. This is the actualization process. By turning the coordinates of thought slowing toward the actualities, our thinking will be closer to reality. "Enlightenment" is reached when angle A becomes zero and our thoughts will fully reflect reality.

The objects are perpendicular to each other because they are mutually exclusive. The actualities are also perpendicular to each other because they are independent. The objects and the actualities belong to different thought spaces. Objects are one-dimensional and actualities are two-dimensional.

Many-Worlds Representation

Reality may be represented by many sets of objects and each set constitutes a complete world. We may have different thinking bases to establish the same reality. For a reality, we may have many different, but equivalent, ways of interpretations.

Therefore, the real world may have many worldviews. Every observer may choose his own most proper set of objects to express his worldview. A world is a set of objects and their interactions.

In a society, we always use our most familiar and complete coordinates to build our organizational systems. For the same purpose, we may have many organizations. This is the basis for a pluralistic society. The Chinese philosopher Zhang Dongsun 張東蓀 labels this as *pluralistic epistemology*.

As shown in the geometric diagram, we may choose different coordinates to represent a reality vector. For example, in a polar coordinate system, a reality vector may be represented as its polar angle and its magnitude.

Lao-tzu uses many examples to elaborate on this principle in the Tao Te Ching. Each chapter describes the principle of Tao using a different set of objects and their proper relations. But all Chapters describe the same principle of Tao.

The Linguistic Model

In the Interaction Model, we have the precise *conceptual* relations between actualities and objects. The main characteristic of actuality is the complementarity of the objects. In this section, we shall discuss a linguistic model as a proper way to describe various concepts in our language. This is a complex philosophical problem, but we can use a scientific model to deal with this issue.

We assume the objects are parts of the common language that we can already share in communication. In the description of actuality, we are faced with a complex structure that cannot be easily reduced to language. The main difficulty in describing the actuality is the interferences produced by the objects within the actuality. The actuality describes the holistic quality or property of the reality. We need to quantify it to have the linguistic expression of the actuality.

Simple and Complex Concepts

In the Interaction Model, we have the conceptual relations between objects and actualities. In a logic model, we need to quantify or reduce all these concepts to language. We first have to distinguish between the *concepts* of objects and the *concepts* of actualities.

- The objects represent our mature and shared experiences that can be reduced to *simple concepts*. We have proper words for these simple concepts. Objects may be directly *quantified* as the conventional words that are understood and can be shared.[1]
- The actualities are *complex concepts*. They are *the superposition* of two *s*imple concepts. When we think of actuality, our thinking is still based on objects, so the two opposite concepts will interfere in our minds. For this reason, actuality cannot be easily expressed in terms of simple language.

---

[1] We may say that, after we recognize the reality as the actualities, these actualities are reified as objects. *Reify* means "to think of or treat something abstract as if it existed as a real and tangible object."

The manifestations of Tao are actualities. As we shall see later, can only be expressed in terms of the vague language of opposite and indeterminate meanings. This is an important conclusion for our understanding of the logic of Tao philosophy: The apparent self-contradiction in the words of Lao-tzu is logically required to describe the true manifestations of Tao.

Quantification of Concepts

Our Linguistic Model is a way to quantify the concepts with language. When we encounter a concept, we try to describe the concept in words, so it can become an *object of knowledge*. This is a complex process in the growth of social, language, and cultural evolution.

In sciences, we have encountered similar issues. The quantification follows a mathematical process to reduce concepts (mathematical functions) to measurable physical properties. For example, the electromagnetic wave is a mathematical function, and the square of that function shows the distribution of the measurable electromagnetic strength.[1] The square of the function naturally contains interferences of all components in that function. In quantum physics, the square of the state function is related to physical measurements. In quantum theory, we call such quantified values the *Expectation Values*.

---

[1] The mathematical functions are often in terms of complex variables and the "square" has a more complicated meaning.

We may use a similar scientific method to quantify actualities. That is, we treat the squares of the actualities as their quantified values. The linguistic relationship between these quantified objects and actualities is the logic model we are looking for. Therefore, the purpose of our linguistic model is to find the logic to describe an actuality in terms of language.

Quantification of Objects

Quantification of a concept is to represent the concept in language. Objects are simple concepts, so quantification of an object can be expressed in common language. Quantification of Wu and Yu is simply the conventional Wu and Yu that have well-defined meanings.

We shall use the following symbols to simplify our discussion: We shall use [x] to represent the square of the function <x>. So we use $[Wu] = |<Wu>|^2$ and $[Yu] = |<Yu>|^2$ Simply said, [Wu] is "with no differences," [Yu] is "with distinct differences."

Quantification of the Actualities

Quantification of the actuality can be expressed in more complex language. According to the quantification process, quantification of an actuality is the square of its function. Therefore, quantifications of Heng Wu and Heng Yu are the square of the functions in Equation (1). The *quantifications* of these actualities may be written as:

Chapter III The Logic of Tao Philosophy   65

$$[\text{Heng Wu}] = \{ a^2 [\text{Wu}] + b^2 [\text{Yu}] \} + a b [\text{Wu*Yu}]$$
$$[\text{Heng Yu}] = \{ a^2 [\text{Yu}] + b^2 [\text{Wu}] \} - a b [\text{Wu*Yu}]$$

Equation 2 Characteristics of the Actualities

Here [Wu] and [Yu] represent the conventional words for the simple objects Wu and Yu. The first two terms are in the curly brackets on the right-hand side of Eq.[2] can be expressed with the words we use to describe Wu and Yu, but the description will be fuzzy because a and b are smaller than 1. The second term [Wu*Yu] represents a new product of two-way interactions between Wu and Yu. This new product is in addition to the two "parts," so the whole is not just the sum of the parts.

A linguistic description of the actuality is given in Equation (2). Equation (2) is the key result of our Linguistic Model. When we describe the actualities in terms of two opposite Wu and Yu, there will be two distinct parts in our descriptions. We have:

- The first part (shown within the curly brackets) can be expressed in terms of our ordinary words [Wu] and [Yu]. This part consists of words with opposite meanings and with reduced clarity (since a, b are less than 1). Therefore, the description of the actualities in words will be *vague* and *self-contradictory*. This part is similar to the usual *Fuzzy Logic*.
- The second part [Wu*Yu] is a product of two-way interferences of Wu and Yu. This term cannot be described by Wu and Yu, because it is a brand new independent product. This part cannot be clearly described by Wu and Yu. This is the *Third World* of Popper.

Equation (2) shows that the description of the actualities, *in our existing language*, will always appear to be "vague, self-contradictory, and indeterminate."

Logical Description of Reality

Equation (2) shows two ways to describe reality. We may read the Equation from left to right: The reality of Tao is revealed as Heng Wu and Heng Yu. When we use Wu and Yu to describe them, they will appear to be vague, self-contradictory, and indeterminate. Lao-tzu describes these two manifestations as the "obscurity upon obscurity" nature of reality. When we read the Equation from right to left, we choose two opposite objects to describe the reality, the result is also "vague, self-contradictory, and indeterminate."

This is the foundation of the Logic of Tao Philosophy. This means that the vague, indeterminate, and self-contradictory words of Lao-tzu are necessary to describe the manifestations of Tao.

Equation (2) represents the complete structure of Lao-tzu's logic system. Such logic structure cannot be represented in the conventional Venn diagram. However, the logic represented by Eq.(2) is similar to the Fuzzy Logic and the Three World Logic combined.

Fuzzy Logic

The first part of Eq. (2) is similar to the usual fuzzy principle. The two opposites may appear with various proportions to represent the whole ($a^2 + b^2 = 1$). The coefficients a, b are determined by the principle of Tao and satisfy the condition for complementarity.

This part of the logic of Tao philosophy is simply the usual Fuzzy Thinking (Kosko1994).

The Third World

The second part is a new object, and cannot be described by the original two objects. However, this part will become a definite object when understood. The science philosopher Karl Popper identifies it as the "third world" in his "three-world system."

Popper (1978) cites an example of such a third world: A piece of artwork is a *definite* creation of an artist in the world. The artwork is neither the artist nor the original world. This third world shows that the whole is not determined only by its parts, there is always something new.

When we describe reality in terms of the existing words, we are always forced to form new concepts and create new words to describe this third world. This is a natural result in the logic of mereology, where the mereological sum is larger than the sum of the parts. Such creativity is driven by the Oneness of nature. We may call it the *Mereological Principle*.[1]

We should note that the third world appears only at the object level. For realists, the objects are real, so the third world is real. For idealists, the actualities are real, so the third world does not exist. These two views are proven to be equivalent in our model.

Language Problem

If we insist on a *positive* and *definite* description of reality without contradiction, then our current language is never adequate and will always demand the creation of new objects to describe the new reality. However, the new language is still dualistic. Such language problem exists in all languages and does not occur only in translation.[2]

---

[1] Hilary Putnam gave an example of three objects. The world of idealism will have three real entities and the world of realism will have seven real entities. (Putnam 1987, p.18). This is consistent with our model.

[2] As pointed out by Wittgenstein, the basic problem in philosophy is the problem of language.

Although our language is inadequate to describe reality, language is still the necessary tool. The problem of language should not become the reason not to discuss Tao. Our language will evolve with our continuing understanding of reality.

The major problem in our interpretation of the *Tao Te Ching* is due to a misunderstanding of the logic of Lao-tzu. It is not just a problem in language or translation but is our habit of dualistic thinking. Linguistic descriptions in Chinese and English are equally vague. However, if the description follows appropriate logic, then the description of reality is not vague.

To describe a new reality, we often have to redefine the existing words with new meanings. As in the quantum theory, many classical definite terms (such as mass and energy) must be modified to be "vague, self-contradictory and indeterminate. The vagueness and uncertainty appear because we think in classical terms. In many cases, new words are coined to represent new concepts, such as an electron, neutron, laser are all created by modern sciences.

As long as our language is dualistic, our ordinary language will remain inadequate. The only remedy is to have complementarity integrated into our language. In the meantime, our thinking habits have to overcome the rigidity of our language.

The Images in Our Brain

Dualism is the simplest way to deal with a whole. This is how we think and may be similar to the structure of our brain.

Our left and right brains provide two parallel functions. We may associate the undifferentiating function of the right brain with Wu that holds the holistic view and associates the left brain with Yu that holds the analytic (differentiated) view. The two brains are not independent and are correlated through the *corpus callosum*, a nerve bundle connecting the two cerebral hemispheres. The two brains interact to maintain the whole view. The function of our whole brain is a complementarity of the two hemispheres.

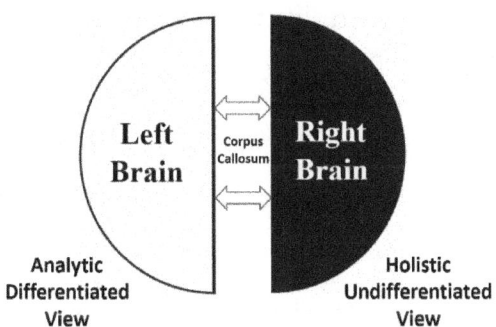

Figure 6 Complementarity of Two Hemispheres

These two complementary brains work in unison and parallel, to preserve wholeness. The two brains reflect the same reality.

Our logic model almost just duplicates the function of the brain. The left and right brains are objects, interconnected by the corpus colosseum. The similarity is obvious. When fully functioning, the right brain is in the state of Heng Wu, and the left brain is in the state of Heng Yu. Every reality is perceived as two equivalent and simultaneous images in our left and right brains.

Summary of the Logic

The purpose of this chapter is to understand the principle in the *Tao Te Ching* and the logic used by Lao-tzu to describe this principle. We may summarize the Logic of Tao Philosophy as:

- The description of reality must consist of vague and contradictory (opposite) statements to cover the whole domain of the reality;
- The description of reality must include indeterminate objects to account for the conceptual interferences within the whole;

These are the two characteristics of the Logic of Tao philosophy. We consider Lao-tzu's description as fuzzy and indeterminate *only* because we think in terms of objects. Such vague, contradictory, and indeterminate descriptions follow the principle of Tao coherently. Lao-tzu's language structure is not arbitrary.

If we can understand the logical structure of Tao philosophy, we can overcome the dualistic linguistic description and the accuracy of Tao itself. Lao-tzu's words have followed this logic earnestly. We should not speculate on the meanings of Lao-tzu's words. His words should be viewed holistically to see the true Tao.

Therefore, we need to build reality out of vague, self-contradictory, and indeterminate language. We need to have a major paradigm shift from thinking at the object level to thinking at the actuality level. This task cannot be easily accomplished. It seems a meditation process to reconstruct the reality from between the lines. We may validate our logic model with the *Tao Te Ching*. The *Tao Te Ching* is the best *experimental observation* of the logic of Lao-tzu.

Part II of this book will recap the major characteristics of this model and correct a few concepts in the traditional Tao philosophy.

Chapter IV
Characteristics of the Tao Logic

No problem is more central to understanding the nature of existence, or knowledge, or values, or logic than the problem of the nature and relations of a whole and the parts, and of wholeness and partiality.

Archie J. Bahm
Metaphysics

If one must use metaphorical language, then let the metaphor be this: the mind and the world jointly make up the mind and the world.

Hilary Putnam
Reason, Truth and History

In Part I, we have developed the *Logic of Tao Philosophy*, and the model reflects our general thinking process. We are accustomed to looking at everything with two opposite objects. Lao-tzu and the Pre-Socratic philosopher Parmenides have warned us not to take these two objects as two separate realities. However, we are lost in many problems.

Parmenides and Lao-tzu describe their views with many examples. Their descriptions are different, but their basic thoughts are very similar. The Buddhists advocate the same principle in the method of negation. However, for two thousand years, their views remain unclear and puzzle us.

In the previous chapters, we have shown how the two opposite concepts complement and support each other. The concept of complementarity is also the ancient philosophical problem of the *parts* and the *whole*. The importance of complementarity is that all realistic concepts must be whole. Only reality can last and can have real meaning. This is what Lao-tzu repeatedly emphasizes in the *Tao Te Ching*. Many misinterpretations and difficulties are due to the error in taking the objects to be real.

As shown in our Linguistic Model, the complementarity of simple conceptual unfortunately produces a complicated language structure. The complementarity of the opposite concepts results in a fuzzy and indeterminate logic of Tao philosophy. Lao-tzu's words are to reflect this logic, but his linguistic logic is often misinterpreted. Now, our model can show the nature of this "obscurity upon obscurity" in Tao.

Although our conclusions are from the analysis of the *Tao Te Ching*, this is the most basic dualism problem in the East and West philosophy. Our discussions may be applied to other philosophical thinking.

The Characteristics at Each Level

Our designation of three levels is only for convenience in our development of the logic model. We need to use words at the object level to describe the manifestations of Tao at the actuality level. The object and the actuality levels have different complexities, but they are *equivalent* descriptions of the same reality. Every level has its clear characteristics.

The Absolute Reality and God

The absolute reality is our immediate apprehension of reality. This reality is perceived before any conscious conditioning of our thought. It is the *unconditioned nature* of nature, or Pu 樸, and is without any structure, but it governs the way we perceive the myriad things.

Lao-tzu designates Tao as One. All myriad things and thoughts should conform to the grand view of this Oneness. The myriad things from the whole of nature should preserve the Oneness of nature.

The holistic manifestation of Tao in the phenomenal world is Non-polarization (無極). However, Lao-tzu identifies this holistic manifestation as "Shen 神" [Ch.60]. A common English translation of this Shen is "God" or "Spirit." The "opposite" of God is ghost 鬼 [Ch.60]. The word Ghost is symphonious and is often symbolized as the Valley 谷.[1]

---

[1] 鬼 Ghost and Valley 谷 have similar pronunciations in Chinese.

Chapter IV Characteristics of Tao Logic

In the *Yi-Chuan* 易傳 as: "God is the uncertainty of Yin and Yang."[1]

The early Western missionaries to China translate this god of Lao-tzu as a divine God. Together with its two manifestations, They identified Tao philosophy as the Trinity. Our systematic model does show this structure of a trinity：Tao and its two manifestations are ontologically equivalent.

In terms of Western philosophical terminology, we may say that Tao is the "Being" and the manifestations are the *beings*. Therefore, Tao is the *ontological ground* for all beings. Therefore, the myriad things obey the order of Tao to show their reality. The interaction laws of this order are Te 德. Thus, the myriad things must obey Tao and Te [Ch.51].

Characteristics of Actualities

In dualistic thinking, there will be two polarized manifestations of reality. Every thinking may start with two opposite objects, which can then complement each other to become actualities. The myriad things of Lao-tzu generally refer to the actualities, but could also mean the objects. When used as actualities, each myriad thing is a whole; if used as objects, each object include its interactions

---

[1] 《繫辭》:「陰陽不測之謂神。」

The myriad things at the actuality level observe the *Principle of Oneness*. The myriad things exist by this principle. When we distinguish the myriad things, we must preserve their wholeness so they can be real, as Lao-tzu says in Chapter 23: "if divided, keep them as whole 曲則全.". This is also observed by Chuang-tzu 莊子 as "The myriad things are numerous, but they are governed by Oneness."

A reality becomes multi-facets without being divisible. Actualities are different, but they are equivalent. As Chuang-tzu 莊子 says, "It is divided, but not divided." We cannot determine which group is more appropriate. This is the *Principle of Equivalence*.

Actualization

Our thinking in terms of objects must be actualized to have reality. This is a very important Paradigm Shift. We must in our minds integrate and harmonize the dualistic objects to form the actualities, and thus subdue the original opposite nature of the objects. Thus we may see the meaning of Lao-tzu words. Lao-tzu describes such harmonization efforts in Chapters 4 and 10 as:

Blunt its sharpness and unravel its entanglements.
Harmonize its lights and blend with its surroundings.

This is an inner process. If we first consider the objects to be real, the actualities are reality at a higher level. Such a process also negates the reality of the objects. For example, in the dualistic thinking of "creation and destruction," an actuality is neither created nor destroyed. This basic concept is the same as the Buddhist philosophy, only worded differently.

Illusions

The Principle of Equivalence ensures that the two manifestations must appear and disappear at the same time, so their *cyclic* transformation is only an illusion. When one manifestation disappears, both manifestations should disappear。 However, when both disappear, it does not become nothing but returns to Oneness.

The Principle of Complementarity ensures that the two objects must appear and disappear at the same time, so "Wu comes from Yu" is an illusion. Besides, "co-arising Yu and Wu" cannot be cyclic. Wu and Yu must appear at the same time. Moreover, when all objects and manifestations disappear, all will return to the Oneness of "god." The world may have no objects or actualities, but it can never become Nothingness. Nothingness is also an illusion.

Trinity

The relationship between the absolute reality and the two manifestations is "the one and the many." The manifestations have wholeness and the reality has Oneness, the relationship is also "Oneness-and-Wholeness." The two manifestations are not truly many, since they are equivalent to each other.

Moreover, the two manifestations represent accurate descriptions of the absolute reality in the phenomenal world. The holistic manifestation of the absolute reality in the phenomenal world is God, so God and its two manifestations are ontologically equivalent, and constitute a Trinity.

The doctrine of Two Truths

Any reality, under dualistic thinking, will produce two actualities that are equivalent to reality. These two actualities exist at the same time and reflect the same *principle* in the reality.

In Tao philosophy, Heng Wu and Heng Yu are two equivalent ways of observing myriad things. Both obey the same principle of Tao, thus constituting a Doctrine of Two Truths. Wu-wei and Yu-wei are two equivalent ways to execute the order of Tao, reflecting the Principle of Equivalence. Chuang-tzu also recognizes the doctrine as Two ways and two manifestations.[1]

From a different view, the actual level and the object level also constitute a Doctrine of Two truths. This is similar to *the Doctrine of Two Truths* of the Buddhist philosopher Nagarjuna in Buddhism. The Conventional Truth is the way of using the interacting objects to describe reality; the Ultimate Truth is the way of using actualities to observe the reality. This kind of Doctrine of Two Truths also appears in the early Greek philosopher Parmenides' *On Nature*.

---

[1] 莊子：兩行、兩見。

Objectification

When our description of an actuality is accepted as matured, it becomes our common language and we may reduce an observed manifestation to a new object. We call this the *objectification* of the manifestation.[1]

Therefore, objectification is the evolution process of knowledge. Our language will evolve with our attempt to describe new manifestations. New knowledge obtained by objectification is mostly built upon the old knowledge. Only in a *revolutionary* paradigm change, a new set of objects may be introduced.

In sciences, quantum theory and relativity are revolutionary changes, so they generate new objects and interaction theories.

Characteristics of the Objects

Our linguistic description of reality is at the object level. The object level is more complicated. Each object can only have reality within its sub-domain. We may introduce interactions to re-integrate these objects back into a whole. Therefore, the interaction is also a necessary object and its reality is only at the object level.

---

[1] If we treat the actualities as *qualities* of the reality and the objects as *quantities*, then objectification is the process of *quantification* of the qualities.

Any group of objects covering the domain of reality may form actualities with different structures to represent the same reality.

The Objects Have Limited Reality

Lao-tzu recognizes that objects may be used as the normal starting point of thinking, but the objects must complement each other to form realistic actualities. Objects are real in their subdomains; but when we view the whole, the objects have no reality.

We communicate mostly with language. For effective communication, we must share a common language and a common platform to communicate the truth effectively and meaningfully. In the logic model, the objects are our common language. Language must be logically correlated to reflect reality. Reality is often beyond words and can be seen only between the lines.

In Western Realism or Materialism, these objects as "real objects." But, in Idealism, the actualities are real. These two ways of thinking are equivalent.

The Objects obey Formal Logic

The objects obey the usual laws of formal logic, such as the law of identity, the law of non-contradiction, the law of excluded middle, and the law of the "negation of negation". These are the logic of our ordinary language and scientific objects. At the object level, the logic is "the opposite of a truth is false." At the actuality level, the proper logic is "the opposite of a truth is another truth." The objects are opposites at the object level; the objects are complementary at the actuality level.

Lao-tzu never denies the traditional logic rules. The traditional logic treats objects as real and does not include the *correlations* between the objects. Complementarity is not part of the formal logic. Lao-tzu tries to steer us away from taking objects as individual and separate realities. The reality can only be recovered with the full complementarity of the objects.

The formal logic is not applicable at the actuality level. The actualities are ontologically equivalent and may have spontaneous transformation. The actualities are internally related; their structure is determined by the correlations of the objects. Such interactions are an integral part of scientific theory. Therefore, the logic model may be applied to philosophy and sciences.

Objects are Social Products

There is no *eternal* or *pre-determined* object in the very beginning. At any time, the objects are *culturally* and *socially* chosen. In any culture, there is always a set of conventional objects as the starting point of all investigations. New objects may be created from the old culture and can change the old culture. All changes are systemic changes.

The objects and their interactions always appear together, change together, and disappear together. When we choose different objects, we will have different interactions. If we change the interactions, the objects will change. The ever-changing nature of the objects and their interactions simply follow the same principle to reflect reality. Nature is like an organic system.

Objects are Non-Being

For no obvious reasons, some scholars consider Yu as being and Wu as non-being. This does not fit in our logic. According to the logic of Tao philosophy, both Wu and Yu should be non-being, because only Heng Wu and Heng Yu are beings. We have to observe the difference, otherwise, the logic becomes confusing.

Objects create Illusion

We are so used to objects and could not overcome the fact that objects have no reality. Many paradoxes are thus created. It is impossible to think that shrinking occurs at the same time within expanding, as Lao-tzu describes in Chapter 36 of the *Tao Te Ching*. In reality, shrinking and expanding are two objects to describe a phenomenon. In reality, the two objects occur within each other, in complementarity.

A Many-to-Many Relation

The actualities and objects have a *many-to-many* relation. However, manifestations and objects are not truly "many," since all manifestations are equivalent and all objects are interrelated. But the many objects are correlated within Oneness, so they are not independently many. At the object level, the whole is not the simple "sum" of the objects; these objects must be properly correlated to describe the whole. Therefore, the interconnectedness between the objects is an integral and necessary component at the object level.

Any change in an object will require changes in all other objects to maintain Oneness and will change the description of all manifestations. A local change will cause a global evolution. Objects and Actualities have "different kinds" of reality. The correlations among the objects will govern the internal structure of the actuality and give rise to interferences of the objects. These new products of interference cannot be described with the original objects and must give rise to new objects.

When we encounter a new reality, we define the objects to cover the domain of reality. We then describe the reality in terms of these objects. When these descriptions are well accepted, these descriptions become new knowledge and are encoded as new objects. Thus, new knowledge depends upon the old knowledge. The selection of our initial set of objects is culturally and socially based. There are no eternal objects.

This also shows a very important "nonlocal effect": A local change will produce global evolution.

The Interactions of the Objects

The objects constitute the static domain of reality at the object level. The interactions are necessary to maintain the principle of Tao at the object level. The interactions integrate all objects into the whole of reality. There is a definite law of these interactions.

The interactions directly reflect the principle of Tao. They represent the power of Tao at the object level. Tao is a principle and interactions are the way to achieve the principle.

The Law of Interactions as *Te*

The interactions between the objects are critical in creating harmony among the objects. We do not know the interactions, but we do know that the sole purpose of the interactions is to reconstruct the whole from the parts.

As in any interaction system, there must be a *law of interactions* to ensure that all objects are in perfect harmony within the whole. We may identify this law of interaction with Te 德.[1]

The Te of an object is the proper way by which the object interacts with all other objects. Each object should act according to this Te to participate in the whole. Although different groups of objects will require different interactions, the law of interactions remains the same. This law governs the external relation of the objects.

At the object level, the interactions are explicit, but at the actuality level, the interactions become the internal relationships within each actuality. And the interaction becomes obscure, and Lao-tzu calls this law of interaction the *Obscure Te* 玄德.

Tao, Te, and Chi form a System

Tao (the principle), Te (laws of interaction), and Chi 氣 (field of harmonizing forces) form a complete system of Tao philosophy. Tao and Te are equivalent concepts： Tao in the overall order and Te is the principle of interaction that preserves Oneness in the phenomenal world. As Lao-tzu states in Chapter 22, the appearances of Te in the phenomenal world reflect the principle of Tao exactly.

---

[1] This principle has also been identified as *li* 理.

As in scientific theories, the interactions are due to a "field" among the objects and the interactions will reflect the characteristics of Chi. Lao-tzu says in Chapter 42: The myriad things carry yin and embrace yang, and Chi is poured over them to attain harmony. *Chi* is the intrinsic force for harmonization of Yin 陰 and Yang 陽 in the myriad things. The characteristics of this field determine the law of interactions, so Chi is closely related to Te. Chi preserves the complementarity of yin and yang, as Te preserves the complementarity of any opposite objects.

In maintaining Oneness, Tao, Te, and Chi are equivalent, are of equal importance, and represent the same reality.

The Harmonization Forces

If we think in terms of actualities, there is no interaction between the actualities. At the object level, because we think in terms of dualistic objects, so we have to use the interactions to maintain wholeness and to eliminate the opposing nature of the objects. The interactions appear as a phantom force, only because we think in terms of dualistic objects. The only function of the interactions is complementarity.

In Western philosophy, such interactions are considered as Love and Strife between the objects. But, in Tao philosophy, the interaction of *Chi* 氣 achieves harmony. Therefore, the interaction created by Chi does not have dualistic nature of strife and love. The complementarity in Chi results in harmony within the actuality.

Teleological Forces

In our logic model, the interactions appear as external forces acting on the objects. The objects are changing due to these interactions and these interactions also change due to changing objects. All objects are in flux and are changing, but are always driven by these external forces that bind them together. Hence, these forces have a definite purpose of guiding all objects to maintain Oneness.

As long as we think in terms of objects, such interaction will naturally appear. They are similar to the teleological force of Aristotle (384-322 BCE). These teleological forces are ubiquitous whenever we observe in terms of the objects in the phenomenal world. This is also the driving force in the process philosophy.

We may view such forces as imposed by Tao on the objects. Lao-tzu has identified this holistic manifestation of Tao as "god 神" [Ch.60]. Therefore, all objects are subject to the power of this "god." This god is not personified and should not be construed to be a theistic god or a material Creator.

At the actual level, this teleological force disappears completely. The actualities have complete independence and freedom.

Manifestations are Equivalent

We cannot describe a reality directly, but all manifestations of reality are *equivalent* representations of the principle of that reality. All actualities are pointers to the same principle. What we use to describe reality are not the reality itself, and the pointers to the reality.

In the model, Heng Wu and Heng Yu are equivalent pointers to the same principle of Tao. They differ only in form and are the same. They are transformations of each other within Oneness. This property has also been observed, e.g., by Hsuen-tzu 荀子 (238 -198 BCE); he says:

> "Difference change in form and not, in essence, is called Transformation (化). Transforming without differentiation is the reality of Oneness." [1]

The two actualities show differences only in their forms, but the principle that produces the actualities is the same. The two "seemingly opposite" actualities always appear together and we cannot take either one of the actualities to be closer to reality.

---

[1] 荀子〈正名〉:"狀變而實無別而為異者,謂之化。有化而無別,謂之一實。"

Therefore, in Tao philosophy, we cannot prefer any object or any manifestation to be closer to reality (Tao). This is very important in Tao philosophy: "The opposite of a truth is another truth." Therefore, we should not prefer any object or actuality. If we show any partiality, we will deviate from Tao.

There is only one principle of Tao. Lao-tzu describes the same principle of Tao with different examples in different Chapters of the *Tao Te Ching,* such as government, war, family, personal cultivation, etc. These examples show the principle of Tao. All actualities are equivalent *ontologically* since they describe the same reality.

Opposite Ways to the Same Goal

One of the key features in Tao philosophy is that a goal can be achieved equally well with two opposite approaches. Based on this, we may follow different paths to search for the same goal without deviating from Tao. It does not matter how a *real* action gets started, both opposite "actions" will be initiated. However, as long as the action is harmonized by the same principle, its results will be equivalent. Execution must follow the principle of Tao.

To Incite the Opposite

At the object level, the opposite objects will appear in complementarity at the same time in dualistic thinking. Any object that appears will automatically induce the appearance of its opposite.

This is hard to understand in traditional thinking. However, this is very natural in the logic model to have complementarity of the opposite objects. For example, when we have the desire to live, there will be room for death [Ch.50, Ch.75]. Living with nature does not seek life or death. To be beyond life and death is called: beyond life and death (出生入死). True living does not consider life and death.

Tao moves the Opposite

Starting with any object will automatically initiate its opposite object to appear. Therefore, to start an action, we may start its opposite action to induce the desired action. There are many examples in the *Tao Te Ching* indicating such subtlety:

> For it to shrink, it must have been already expanded (36)
> Teaching without word and benefit with Wu-wei can seldom be matched by anything else in the world. (43)
> Misfortune is where fortune lies. Fortune is where misfortune hides. (58)

These actions are at the object level. The two opposite actions exist complementarily and are always co-arising.

The One and the Many

The logic of Tao Philosophy deals with the logical relation between the *parts* and the *whole*, i.e., between the many and the one relationship of Aristotle. This is also an ancient philosophical issue in the West.

Our model can shed definite light on this problem. In our model, the relation between absolute reality and the actualities is "one and many." But the many actualities are equivalent representations for the same reality. Therefore, the many actualities are not truly many. In a dualistic system, we have a trinity represented ontologically by two actualities and the absolute reality. This is the true meaning of "one and many."

The one and the many is also a convenient way to describe reality and the phenomenal world. The reality is one and the phenomenal world is many. But the one and the many are both the way of Tao.[1]

---

[1] 莊子大宗師第六：其一也一；其不一也一。其一與天為徒；其不一與人為徒。天與人不相勝也，是之謂真人。

The Tao Te Ching is not Self-Contradiction

The most important conclusion of our logic model is that the words of Lao-tzu may appear paradoxical and self-contradictory, but they are logically constructed to reflect the true principle of Tao. The self-contradiction in the *Tao Te Ching* is only the way to express the whole reality of the actualities.

What appears as self-contradiction is that we are unable to overcome the habits of thinking in terms of the objects and take objects to be real, thus unable to understand Lao-tzu's descriptions of the manifestations of Tao. After we understand this logic, we can see how Lao-tzu uses the complementarity of objects to construct actualities, and all chapters of the *Tao Te Ching* reflect the same Principle of Tao.

We cannot easily classify Lao-tzu as a mystic with self-contradiction. Lao-tzu affirms parallel realities representing an absolute reality. He is not an absolute monist. Neither, he thinks that there are two *separate* realities, so he is not a relativist. Nor does Lao-tzu proclaim a nihilism that denies all reality. For Lao-tzu, the reality is the Oneness of nature, but we need to use conventional objects to describe the manifestations of this reality.

Dualistic Fallacies

Most spurious debates and paradoxes in the interpretation of the *Tao Te Ching* may be attributed to a failure in observing the reality of the issues, and fall into dualistic fallacies.

For example, in Tao philosophy, we have debates on Wu and Yu (有無之爭). Wu and Yu are objects without reality. The two real Heng Wu and Heng Yu are equivalent, so there is no need to debate. Therefore, the traditional debate about Wu and Yu is a case of dualistic fallacy, and a proper understanding of the logic of Tao philosophy can avoid falling into such *dualistic fallacies*. Whitehead comments that we misplace reality at the object level.

Such dualistic fallacy seems to be the *original sin* in philosophical discussions. It is very hard to avoid dualism. Our discussions often start and end with dualism, and we are unable to stay with the obscure actualities. Often the problem is in the way we think.

We often ask, "If reality is unchanging, why is ...?" In such a question, we already assume duality (changing/unchanging) is meaningful, so we are already lost. It is almost impossible to avoid dualism, but the logic of Tao philosophy can help us maintain wholeness in our dualistic thinking and return to thinking methods that have reality.

The concept of Heng in the first chapter of the *Tao Te Ching* is a key concept to avoid dualistic fragmentation. Heng refers to Oneness, wholeness, and truth. At all times, we should think in terms of actualities, and forever avoid the appearance of the characteristic of the objects.

Creativity

One of the most important concepts in Tao philosophy is the ceaseless creativity of "things" (生生不息) in nature. These things may refer to the objects and the corresponding actualities. In our model, there is a definite creativity process, the things are not created randomly.

Creativity can sustain only when what we create is a reality. That is, we can create only when we return to the state of Oneness, where we have infinite choices of different sets of objects to describe reality. In other words, Oneness will allow unlimited creativity; different objects can be constantly created

Creativity by Groups

Objects are constantly created as a group during our pursuit of reality since the old objects are always insufficient or we have perceived new actualities. All objects are based on Oneness as background. The objects can emerge as though they create themselves by conforming to Oneness.

In this ceaseless creativity, both objects and actualities change simultaneously as a group. There is no individual creation alone. Any individual change will initiate changes in the group. All changes are subject to the Oneness of the group. This is probably what Lao-tzu means by: "one should not try to stand ahead of the world."[1] We are all related and should remain submerged in the whole without standing out from others.

Actualities and objects co-arise in our minds. New actualities may be revealed to us, but our perceptions are influenced by the objects already in our minds. We may also select a new group of objects spontaneously as though they were created by Tao.

---

[1] Chapter 67: The third treasure of Tao is humility (modesty, respect for others). Humility is being modest or respectful. Literal translation is "dare not to be in front of others in the world (不敢為天下先)."

Being and Becoming

"Being and Becoming" is an ancient philosophical issue. As seen by the Greek philosopher Heraclitus, the group of objects is ever *becoming* at the object level. However, the group of actualities behaves like *beings*, as seen by Parmenides. The relation between Being and Becoming has been a problem in Western philosophy.

In our model, *becoming* and *being* are not in conflict; they are two equivalent views of the same reality at different levels. The actualities are beings, and the objects are forever becoming. The debate on "being and becoming" is only a dualistic fallacy. It is like a Western version of the debate on "Wu and Yu."

An actuality is a being. However, an object cannot become a *being* by itself. All objects must participate complementarily to become a being. When the objects change, the internal structure of the beings will change; however, the reality represented by the beings does not change. However, the beings still represent the same reality. Their nature has not changed.

Language Evolution

As shown in this logic model, our words (objects) are never sufficient for describing reality. When we describe reality with *words*, the reality will appear vague, self-contradictory, and indeterminate. However, if we can overcome the limits of the words and focus on the actualities as a whole, the reality will be clear and true.

Chapter V New Interpretations

> *The intuition of duration [i.e., the flux of experience (the ultimate reality)], when it is exposed to the rays of the understanding ... quickly turns into fixed, distinct, and immobile concepts.*
>
> Henri Bergson,
> An Introduction to Metaphysics

For two thousand years, we have denied that the *Tao Te Ching* is logical. This has created the widest imagination in its interpretation. Countless paradoxes and self-contradiction have plagued our understanding of Tao philosophy. In this historical background, we are naturally ready to accept that the *Tao Te Ching* has no definite principle.

However, we are certain that these views are incorrect. Our discussions clearly show that the *Tao Te Ching* has a clear logical structure. If we can apply this logic in our thinking, many traditional contradictions can be eliminated, and we can have a consistent interpretation of the *Tao Te Ching*.

In this Chapter, we shall highlight how this logic model can eliminate major logical errors in the interpretation of the *Tao Te Ching*. This includes the complementarity of Wu and Yu, equivalence between Wu-wei and Yu-wei, fundamental mysteries of Tao, and the process philosophy of Tao. These are important concepts that should be established in Tao philosophy.

Relationship of Wu and Yu

Wu and Yu are dualistic objects used to describe myriad things. In logic, they are symmetric, co-arising, and complementary. The error in the traditional view has taken Wu to be more fundamental than Yu and assumed Yu can come from Wu. For thousands of years, despite the known logical conflicts with co-arising of Wu and Yu, "Yu comes from Wu" has been the cornerstone of the traditional Tao philosophy.

In our model, the symmetry and complementary relationship of Wu and Yu is clear evidence that "Yu" cannot come from "Wu." We have to treat Wu and Yu on an equal footing. The complementarity of the two opposite objects is the basic structure in dualism.

Chapter V New Interpretations

Source of Traditional Misinterpretation

The traditional notion that "Yu comes from Wu" is based on a segment of Chapter 40 of the traditional *Tao Te Ching:* "The myriad things come from Yu, and Yu comes from Wu." However, this verse appears differently in the Guodian version,[1] which shows this verse as: "The myriad things come from Yu, and come from Wu." It is clear that Wu and Yu appear on equal footing, without the indication that "Yu comes from Wu." We shall show that "Yu comes from Wu" is a misinterpretation.

These two versions differ only by a single Chinese character "Yu" which is repeated in the traditional text. Such textual repetition is common in ancient Chinese texts and in general, does not carry additional meaning. The Yu in the traditional text is superficial.[2] Therefore, the traditional text and the Guodian text have the same meaning.

However, such an important textual difference has not been noticed. A more obvious mistake of the traditional interpretation is that it takes only the second half of the traditional text - "Yu comes from Wu" - as an independent concept. This takes a part to be the whole. For this reason, we believe that the traditional interpretation is not well-founded.

---

[1] This Guodian version (郭店楚簡) was unearthed in 1993. It is the earliest extant version of the *Tao Te Ching* (300 BCE..

[2] The repetition of the trailing word is common writing style known as textual Transfer (層遞) , Returning (回文), and Pointing (頂針).

In the Mawangdui version, Wu and Yu are both related to myriad things. On the contrary, Wang Bi identifies Wu with the origin of heaven and earth and Yu with the source of the myriad things."[1] Therefore, Wu is identified with absolute reality and Yu with the phenomenal world. Since Wang Bi, the relationship between Wu and Yu has been a controversial topic in Tao philosophy.

Complementarity of Wu and Yu

In the *Tao Te Ching*, Wu and Yu must be treated as complementary pairs. Lao-tzu uses many such symmetric pairs in the *Tao Te Ching* to show the principle of Tao. The most outstanding example of the Wu-Yu pair is in Chapter 11. If we assume that Yu comes from Wu, this Chapter is perplexing and awkward. But, by keeping the Wu-Yu as complementary, the interpretation of this Chapter is very logical:

---

[1] Wang Bi Chapter 1: 無、名天地之始；有、名萬物之母。

1   When thirty spokes unite on one hub,
    It is the "Wu and Yu," that makes the wagon useful.
2   When clay is molded into a vessel,
    It is the "Wu and Yu," that makes the vessel useful.
3   When doors and windows are cut out,
    It is the "Wu and Yu," that make the room useful.
4   Therefore,
    Yu provides the support;
    Wu provides the usefulness.

The above parsing shows the Complementarity of Wu and Yu. In this example, Wu refers to the empty central hole of the wheel and Yu to the actual spokes. By treating "Wu and Yu" as asymmetric and complementary pairs, the whole chapter can be interpreted consistently and naturally.

The concluding statement that "Yu provides the support; Wu provides the usefulness" emphasizes such pairwise complementarity. In this Chapter, the realities are functional wagon, vessels, and rooms.

Wu-Wei and Yu-Wei

The difficulties in interpreting Wu-wei and Yu-wei are influenced by the traditional interpretations of Wu and Yu. We are not certain when the symmetry between Wu and Yu is lost in the traditional interpretation. The very earlier interpretations of Chuang-tzu, Huei-tzu, and Huang Lao, maintained the symmetry of Wu and Yu. But, the symmetry was lost in subsequent interpretations.

At the actual level, Wu-wei and Yu-wei are "the Way according to *Heng* Wu" and "the Way according to *Heng* Yu," respectively. When leading, one should act with Wu-wei, which is an undifferentiating altruism act. When executing a task, one should act with Yu-wei, which is differentiating and all-encompassing act. The two obey the same principle of Tao. In logic, Heng Wu and Heng Yu are equivalent, since both conform to the same principle of Tao.

Recovering the Earlier Views

Traditional interpretations prefer Wu-wei and greatly misunderstand Yu-wei. This needs overall re-appraisals. But, the very early scholars of Tao recognized that Wu-wei and Yu-wei are of equal importance. Wu-wei and Yu-wei must complement each other to complete the system of Tao. Therefore, Wu-wei and Yu-wei have been *correctly* interpreted in the early history of Tao philosophy. Our proposal is only to recover the early interpretation. These ancient examples are:

- In Chuang-tzu's *Tao of Heaven* (4th-century BCE), we have "Those above should act with Wu and develop the world; those below should act with Yu and can serve the world. This is the unchanging way. "
- In Huang-Lao school, Tung Chung-shu (179 – 104 BCE) also writes that "The lord is expected to act with Wu, and the subordinate is to act with Yu."
- Han Yin (200 -130 BCE) also states in the Principle of Ruling by Able Lords (賢君治世), that the basic principle of Huang-Lao politic is "The Lord's way is Wu-wei; the Subordinate's way is Yu-wei."

Therefore, Wu-wei is the proper way to lead and Yu-wei the proper way to execute. However, Wu-wei and Yu-wei require the same ability to follow the principle of Tao. Whoever can execute Wu-wei will also be able to execute Yu-wei and vice versa.

Both ways are parallel and necessary efforts to build a Grand System of Tao. Therefore, Lao-tzu does not prefer Wu-wei. Both actions follow the same principle and neither has a higher value.

Demarcation of Wu-wei and Yu-wei

- Man of the utmost benevolence acts according to Wu.
- Man of utmost righteousness acts according to Yu.

The two actions are parallel and follow the same principle. We can freely switch from Wu-wei to Yu-wei and vice versa, according to the states of affairs. A leader may be led; the follower may also lead. The change is only the ways, but not the principle. Lao-tzu does not prefer Wu-wei.

Traditional downplay of Yu-wei

The traditional interpretations take Wu as the proper representation of Tao, and thus often downplay Yu. Tradition often mistakes Yu-wei as actions that deviate from Tao or against Tao. This is due to the traditional misunderstanding of Yu.

From our logic analysis, there is no justification to downplay Yu or Yu-wei. Yu-wei should be interpreted as the action that pays attention to the individual objects with the proper bounds of the whole. Yu-wei is also according to Tao. Wu-wei and Yu-wei cannot be easily distinguished because they follow the same principle.

Logically, Wu-wei and Yu-wei must occur at the same time, to establish the grand system of Tao in the phenomenal world.[1] Traditionally Confucianism emphasizes Yu-wei, but Tao philosophy should also restore the importance of Yu-wei. We should not treat Lao-tzu as anti-Confucianism.

The Mysteries of Tao

The purpose of our model is not to eliminate the mystery of Tao, but to discover the true mystery of Tao. What are the true mysteries of Tao? Tao philosophy has so many mysteries, because we think in terms of objects and cannot properly understand *Tao Te Ching*.

The core mystery of Tao includes the complementarity of the objects, the definiteness of actualities, the relationship between the actualities, and the inadequacy of language. Tao philosophy shows naturally the logic and mystery of the Doctrine of Two Truths and the Trinity. We also show why Tao is omnipresent in the world. These are problems of our thinking logic and are the mysteries of the East and the West philosophy.

---

[1] Chapter 28: Thus, the Grand System can form without fragmentation. 故大制無割。

Most logical mysteries are man-made, and the reason is due to our habitual thinking about reality, in terms of dualistic objects. We are truly lost when we consider the objects as realistic entities, and thus cannot maintain holistic thinking of realistic actualities. Holistic thinking will show the complementary structure of the objects.

This is a very general logic problem. Parmenides and the Buddha used different languages to point out the same problem, and have also provided ways to avoid the problem. Our model can eliminate such logical mysteries and allow us to enter the Garden of Eden where there is no fragmented dualistic thinking (such as good and evil).

Complementarity of Objects

Much of the mysteries of Tao can be attributed to the fuzziness of its manifestations. It is fuzzy only because we habitually think in terms of dualistic opposite objects and do not use proper logic to reconstruct the clear actualities. This makes us unable to avoid the fallacy of dualism.

The only purpose of objects is to complement each other to show the characteristics of actualities. Objects are only parts of reality and must complement. However, we often take objects to be real; even worst, we may take objects to be reality.

For example, we mistake Wu and Yu as real. Thus created many mysteries of Pro-Wu thinking and the reactions of Pro-Yu. Thee Debates of Yu and Wu continues for 2000 years. Some scholars treat Wu as Tao and create the asymmetry of Wu and Yu.

In modern sciences, Relativity deals with the complementarity of time and space, and Quantum Theory with the complementarity of wave and particle. Therefore, the mysteries are much the same. We share the same *core* mystery of complementarity of two opposite concepts. Many mysteries of Tao are not directly related to modern science but may be understood in the same manner.

Complementarity is to harmonize two opposite objects, rather than to abandon two opposite objects and return to the center. Logically, returning to the center is impossible, since the center does not exist. What we need is to restore the whole, instead to search for the center.

Realities are unambiguous

Complementarity of the objects gives rise to the *obscurity* of actualities, but this is because we think in terms of objects. If we think at the actuality level, the actuality itself will be unambiguous.

Language is objects. Linguistic descriptions of the actuality will naturally be vague, self-contradictory, and indeterminate. The manifestations of Tao have fleeting nature. This is also because we think in terms of objects. Therefore, we have to overcome the limitations of our dualistic language to go beyond the objects and preserve the "obscurity" of the manifestations.

Spontaneous Transformation

The relation between the actualities is also mysterious because it is beyond our common dualistic thinking. These two seemly different manifestations represent the same principle of Tao.

The two manifestations of Tao are *simultaneous* and *parallel*, so there is no transition between the two. They are internally related. Although with different structures, Heng Wu and Heng Yu are indistinguishable essences. As Lao-tzu says in Chapter 58 that "There is no stability; certainty becomes an uncertainty; kindness becomes unkindness."

The transformation between actualities occurs spontaneously, effortlessly, and unexpectedly. Transformation is "a state change without differentiation." In transformation, no object is eliminated or created, since all objects are always in all manifestations. The switch is by *internal re-organization*. Changes in actualities are illusions and superficial.

In Heng Wu, we do not treat individual objects with any preference, and all objects will maintain their harmony in the wholeness with implicit order. In Heng Yu, all objects are differentiated and all objects are bound by the wholeness with explicit order. In either case, all objects are present and remain harmonized internally with the profound Te 玄德.

In practice, we often wonder between Heng Wu and Heng Yu. As long as we can maintain Oneness, we may have freedom in transformation, without any effort. This is true freedom. Any holding to any object or manifestation is a deviation from Tao.

Omnipresence of Tao

We always feel the existence of Tao. Behind the myriad things, there is an omnipresent force. This reminds us of a question in the West: why is there always something, instead of nothing?

All this is because we think in terms of objects. But the wholeness of nature is still controlling the objects in our minds. All objects seem to be under teleological forces to gather in the wholeness.

The interactions bind these objects together as One, according to the principle of Tao. Therefore, we sense these interactions as the teleological forces acting on each object. Objects are always under the influence of Tao. As expressed by Heraclitus: "Every creature is driven to pasture with a blow." All objects are under the power of Tao; we feel that Tao is omnipresent.

At the object level, the power of Tao is explicit. At the actuality level, this power is internalized inside the actualities, so the actualities are free with no external force. In practice, we will not be able to maintain such a harmonious state and some objects and interactions will always emerge in our minds. Our consciousness will again become aware of the power of Tao.

Whenever we deviate from Tao (Oneness), objects and interactions will emerge to restore Oneness. Therefore, we feel that Tao is omnipresent.

Common Logical Errors

With the help of a logic model, we can eradicate many errors in the traditional interpretations of the *Tao Te Ching*. The following are the most common errors. This includes misplacing the root of Tao, taking objects as real entities, the cyclic transformation of manifestations, etc.

These errors are due to confusion in logic and are the results of thinking in terms of objects.

The Root of Tao Philosophy

The traditional Tao philosophy treats the object Wu as the root of Tao philosophy and even takes Wu to be Tao. The error is to take an *object* to be the absolute reality. We cannot even take Heng Wu to be Tao, excluding Heng Yu. Similarly, heaven cannot be Tao since heaven and earth are two manifestations of Tao. Tao follows nature and nature includes heaven and earth.

In terms of Being and beings, we may treat Tao as Being and the actualities as *beings*, but we should not treat Wu and Yu as *beings*, since they lack wholeness to be real. Many scholars improperly designate Yu as *being* and Wu as *non-being*.

With the same logic, we may resolve the paradox of Gongsun Long 公孫龍 (320-250 BCE) who stated: "White horse is not horse." The absolute reality is "horse" and its two manifestations are "white horse" and "non-white horse." It is clear that "white horse" is an object that cannot be the reality "the horse." According to our model, Gongsun Long's statement is logical and is not a paradox.

Tao Philosophy is Ontology. It is a very fundamental law that must be observed in all aspects of philosophy. Some scholars associate *The Tao Te Ching* with politics, government, wars, human relations, etc. The fact is that these are examples in the Tao Te Ching to illustrate the principle. Lao-tzu only emphasizes how to preserve reality in our discussions.

Softness and Tenderness

We often mistake actualities as objects and thus fall into dualistic fallacy. It is clear that Lao-tzu prefers softness and tenderness, but we often misplace such softness and tenderness *at the object level* and claim that Lao-tzu prefers soft and tender "objects." What Lao-tzu prefers are the actualities, which have harmonized the strong and fragmented nature of the objects. Only actualities are soft and tender.

Lao-tzu uses infant, or water, to show the quality of "soft and weak" in reality. An infant has a non-discriminating attitude that are qualities of the actuality states. Lao-tzu also uses feminine, or maternity, to represent resourcefulness and creativity of wholeness. By doing so, he certainly does not prefer the female to male at the object level.

For Lao-tzu, the opposite objects always co-arise and are in complementary states at all times. He will certainly not prefer one object over the other. We may think in terms of objects, but we should not hold on to any object and deviate from the principle of Tao.

Cyclic Transformation is Illusion

In dualistic thinking, we often use *cyclic transformation* to describe the co-arising nature of two opposite objects. In such cyclic transformation, something is born all the time. An object becomes another object. Such a cyclic view seems natural because we habitually think of one object at a time. However, such cyclic transition is an illusion because the two opposites must co-exist at all times.

Yu can't come from Wu, because Yu and Wu must co-exist at all times. There are no separate events as *becoming* and *being* in a phenomenon. We should avoid treating any complementary objects as two alternating realities. The "Chicken and egg" problem is another well-known paradox that appears when two objects are treated as separate realities.

Lao-tzu advises against separating any individual object of the harmonious whole; such separation will lead to decay of Oneness. He says, "Fish should not leave the deep creek."[1] Anything that appears as an object from an actuality cannot last: "the rigid leads to an end."[2]

---

[1] Chapter 36: 魚不可脫於淵。

[2] Chapter 76: Strength is inferior; tenderness is favored. (強大居下，柔弱居上。)

Actuality is not in the Middle

Actuality is not to eliminate the opposite objects, but to include them. Avoiding the two extreme objects is not to move to the center, but rather to accommodate the extremes.

Every dualistic thinking has two levels. At the object level, there is no middle between the objects (exclusive middle); at the actuality level, both actualities contain both objects and are whole. Therefore, in dualistic thinking, there is no center. In fact, "returning to the center" is to return to wholeness.

Illusion of Time

The relationship of "past, present, and future" is a Trichotomy. The illusion of time is also a major issue in philosophy. We may use the same logic model.

Time should be treated as a whole and not be taken as instantaneous moments. Fragmented time periods, such as past, present, and future, are the objects used to describe time. Actual time should simultaneously include "past, present, and future" to be a whole. The transition of the time is also an illusion - it is an illusion of transformation of the objects.

Our model may be extended to analyze time. All fragmented objects of time must be harmonized, mixed, and completely complemented before they can be real. See more discussion about time in Appendix A: Living in Now.

Wisdom and Knowledge

Knowledge and wisdom are also a kind of dualistic thinking. Often we think Lao-tzu is against knowledge or even wisdom; this is perplexing. We may also resolve this controversy with our model. Wisdom is actuality and knowledge is an object. Therefore, wisdom is a coherent set of correlated knowledge.

Lao-tzu warns us against relying on knowledge without proper correlations. When wisdom is divided, the knowledge must be held as an integral whole.[1] Lao-tzu simply advocates against taking fragmented knowledge as wisdom.

Lao-tzu is not anti-knowledge. He urges us to seek both knowledge and wisdom. In Chapter 48, Lao-tzu says that, in learning, our knowledge improves when we have more (The Way of Yu). In seeking Tao, our wisdom improves when we rely lesser on the objects (The Way of Wu).

---

[1] Chapter 23: In division, maintain it as a whole; (曲則全)

In the *Tao Te Ching*, wisdom 知 is whole, and knowledge 智 is part. It is interesting to note that knowledge is written as wisdom lasting over a day 日. Knowledge changes daily and can become useful only when they are integrated and correlated as a whole, in which case, correlated knowledge is wisdom. Therefore knowledge and wisdom can always exist together.

Seeking knowledge and wisdom represents proper learning; both should be pursued. When Lao-tzu urges us to "abandon knowledge," he only means to go beyond fragmented knowledge and to have holistic knowledge that is wisdom.

Ames and Hall coin the term *Wu-forms* to describe the various actions or states associated with Wu (Ames & Hall, 2003). To be consistent with our model, Wu-forms should be associated with Heng Wu, and not the object of Wu so we can avoid dualistic fallacy.

In most occurrences, "Wu" in the *Tao Te Ching* does not simply mean "without" or "no." Wu is not a simple negation.

To avoid the dualistic fallacy, Wu should refer to Heng Wu. For example, "Wu-wei" is the impartial action; Wu-wisdom 無知 is "Non-discriminating Wisdom"; "Wu-desire" "Unconditioned desire"; and "Wu-heart" is the "Impartial Heart," etc. All these Wu-forms do not refer to Wu as an object but as actuality Heng Wu.

The Process Philosophy of Tao

We may also view Tao philosophy as an effort to attain reality in the phenomenal world, i.e., by always constructing actualities from objects. This is the actualization process that was discussed in Chapter III. The actualization process in general will take an infinite number of steps to complete.

The multi-step actualization process is essentially the process of Whitehead (1978). In sciences, such a process is essentially the same as the perturbation theory where perturbations are harmonized through a series of stages. This also shows that philosophy and science have the same thinking bases.

Multi-step Actualization

In a multi-step actualization process, we have different sets of objects with different interactions at each step. This multi-step process may be shown in Fig. 7. Here we assume three actualization steps; each step is identified by a group and a level. The objects in every step harmonize part of the interactions to form intermediate actualities. After the intermediate actualities are *objectified*, they will become the objects in the next step of actualization.

In each step, there are residual interactions to be harmonized. The interactions will diminish gradually until they are completely harmonized. The final actualities will then be free from any interactions.

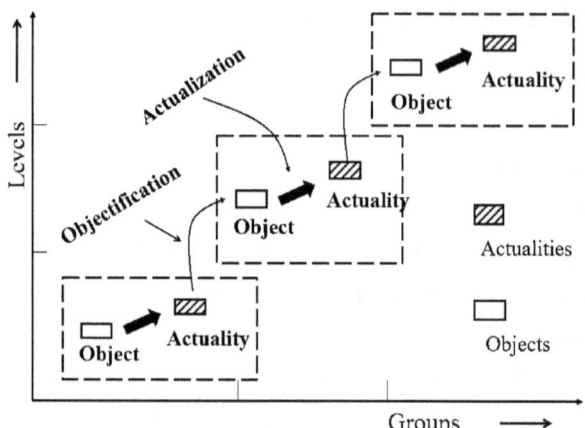

Figure 7 Multi-step Process Philosophy

During each step, the number of objects may increase, decrease, or change completely. Although the objects may change, the principle of Tao remains the same in each step. The final actualities represent the absolute reality *in the phenomenal world*. Every step is an effort to build a more realistic dualism. This is not to eliminate dualism; there are still two actualities at the end. The last step is to form a Sacred Trinity. The two final actualities form a Doctrine of Two Truths. Beyond the phenomenal world, these actualities disappear completely back into Oneness.

Chapter V New Interpretations

The actualization process in Fig. 7 is reversible. We may start with the actualities at the highest level and start to articulate the actualities with objects. In this process, we *articulate* actualities as revelations into objects (words) at every step until we reach the lowest step. At each step, the actuality is constructed as *complementarity* of the dualistic objects. In the next step, the two actualities become the new objects to create new actualities. The structure of the new actuality is the same *complementarity* pattern of the new objects. The structure of the complementarity of objects is endless.

The multi-step process represents a spiritual hierarchy where more and more interactions between the objects are harmonized at each intermediate level. The actualization at each level *internalizes* some additional interaction and represents spiritual growth at each level. All interactions represent the drive to full realization.

Levels and Groups in the *Tao Te Ching*

In the *Tao Te Ching*, Lao-tzu explicitly defines five levels and five groups in the steps to seek Tao. Each step is identified with a level and group, with different objects and interactions. All steps conform to the same principle of Tao and have equivalent reality.

Five Levels

Lao-tzu defines five levels: Tao 道, Te 德, Ren 仁 (benevolence), Yi 義 (righteousness), and Li 禮 (ritual), in Chapter 38:[1]

> Deviating from Tao, we rely on Te.
> Deviating from Te, we rely on Ren.
> Deviating from benevolence, we rely on Yi.
> Deviating from righteousness, we rely on Li.

According to this level structure, if we lose the ability to observe Oneness with Tao at a level, we may rely on a lower level to recover. We can synchronize with the lower level to recover. Each lower level is less integrated and the interactions between the objects are more explicit. By reaching harmony at a level, we may be able to resynchronize with Tao at a higher level.

---

[1] Chapter 38: 故失道而後德，失德而後仁，失仁而後義，失義而後禮。

Tao will be most effective when we can synchronize with Tao at each level, even at the lost levels (Ren, Yi, and Li) as shown in Chapter 21.[1] The principle of Tao is always active at all levels.

Five Groups

Lao-tzu identifies the five groups: Self, Family, Village, Country, and the World in Chapter 54[2] Lao-tzu characterizes Te in each group as "genuine, plentiful, enduring, abundant, and universal." Each group is characterized by its Te. All these Te will conform to the same principle of Tao.

Tao as Philosophy of Organism

The system of Tao consists of a complex of complexes under the same principle. The actualities at each step are *complexes* of different objects at that step. All complexes at different stages of actualization may co-exist under the same principle. This means that Tao will cover all levels and all groups without abandoning anyone.[3]

---

[1] Chapter 21: 同於德者，道亦德之；同於失者，道亦失之。

[2] Chapter 54: 以身觀身，以家觀家，以鄉觀鄉，以邦觀邦，以天下觀天下。

[3] Chapter 27: A sage always helps people, without abandoning anyone. (聖人恆善救人，而無棄人。)

The goal of the process of Tao philosophy is not to eliminate all objects, but to maintain the harmonious relationship of all objects at all steps. This is reflected in the *Tao Te Ching* as "letting all be whatever they are." For example, we let "some lead and some follow; some grow and some fail."[1] In other words, Tao philosophy does not pursue a single absolute reality, by eliminating all others.

The Grand System of Tao allows for a system of plurality to represent the absolute reality, similar to the *Philosophy of Organism* of Whitehead. A pluralistic society is a super complex formed by many complexes and all complexes are properly related to each other.

The Three Levels of Thinking

The logic model is common. In Chinese philosophy, we have many similar multi-level models. For example, Wang Bi 王弼 uses three levels: (1) idea 意, (2) symbols/images 象, and (3) words 言. The idea is the reality; the symbols are actualities; the words are the objects. Shao Yong 邵雍 (1011-1077) characterizes the levels in the *Book of Changes* as (1) God 神, (2) Enumeration 數 and the symbols 象, and (3) the objects 器. Wen-tzu 文子 also uses Tao 道, Form 形, and Object 器 as three levels.

---

[1] Chapter 29: (物或行或隨；或噓或吹；或強或贏；或培或墮。)

Chuang-tzu compares language and ideas to fish traps and the fish. He says, "The fish trap exists, because of the fish; once you have caught the fish, you can forget the trap. Words exist, because of meaning; once you have gotten the meaning, you can forget the words."

Hsuan-tzu 荀子 also discusses *name* 名 and *actuality* 實. He describes the process as: "Names 名 are used when the reality 實 itself is not clearly understood. Combinations of names are used when single names alone are not understood. Explanations are used when combinations of names alone are not understood. Discourses are used when simple explanations alone are not understood."

Our three-level model may also be identified implicitly in the Epistemological Pluralism of Zhang Dongsun 張東蓀 (1886-1962) and the logic model of Jin Yuelin 金玉霖 (1895-1988).

Chapter VI Summary

*While I am reasonably convinced that my view is the correct one,
I shall add that I am by no means certain that it is.*

Hilary Putnam
Mind, Language, and Reality

As said by Aristotle, "The least initial deviation from the truth is multiplied later a thousandfold." A simple logical error in Tao philosophy has now become a big issue between the East and West philosophies. This error is not committed by Lao-tzu, but by the historical interpretations. Adler (1985) classifies it as "Fallacy of reductionism". This kind of philosophical error is to "assign much greater reality to the parts of an organized whole than to the whole itself; or even worse, maintaining that only the ultimate parts have reality and that the whole they constitute is mere appearances, or even illusionary."

Chapter VI Summary

Parmenides, Aristotle, the Buddha, and Lao-tzu have pointed clearly out such errors. But philosophers are still unable to overcome such obvious errors.

The important conclusion of this book is: Lao-tzu is an authentic Chinese ancient philosopher. He describes the principle of Tao in the Tao Te Ching. He emphasizes that we have to maintain wholeness in our thinking. He has clear logical thinking and shows that Tao philosophy is about seeking the nature of reality. His basic thinking is a way to resolve the fallacy of reductionism.

This result is indeed surprising because it is in direct contradiction to the 2000-year old traditional view. This is well beyond what we have expected when I started this project more than a decade ago. This conclusion is a major "turn" in our concept of Tao philosophy. The logic of Tao philosophy can now be shown systematically. The *Tao Te Ching* can be interpreted on a logical framework. The most important is that we have discovered the original intent of Lao-tzu.

Tao as a Common Philosophy

Tao philosophy is an ancient philosophy on nature. We no longer need to accept Tao philosophy as a mysterious *Chinese* philosophy. Tao is an ancient philosophy that is very similar to many other East and West philosophies on nature. Tao philosophy can be analyzed on the same platform with Western thinking and logic.

The traditional mysteries are due to historical interpretations that ignore proper logic. We are lost in mystery because of logical error. We not only have not corrected this minor error but also even extend it into a distortion of the thinking process of a whole civilization.

Tao philosophy deals with the most fundamental question in philosophy: *The First Principle*. It is a philosophy of nature. The thoughts of Lao-tzu may be applied to many philosophical topics, but many topics discussed in the Tao Te Ching are just examples.

Lao-tzu never thinks that his articulation is easy to understand. With traditional thinking, his words are indeed fuzzy and self-contradictory. He even says, "If not ridiculed at, it could not be Tao." (Chapter 41)

Lao-tzu's observations deserve our careful attention; we cannot ridicule him and treat his words as fragments of ancient philosophy.

Chapter VI Summary

For a long time, we have mistaken Tao philosophy as a unique *Chinese* philosophy that is quite different from other philosophies. But our analysis shows that Tao philosophy is fundamentally the same as other philosophies. The principle of Tao is similar to Parmenides' Oneness, Heraclites' Changes, Indian Trinity philosophy, and the Buddha's or Nagarjuna's "Non-dualistic principle." We see the logic of the Doctrine of Two Truth and Trinity in Tao philosophy.

We have benefitted from all other philosophies in our final breakthrough in the search for the principle of Tao. These philosophers express the same principle in different ways. It would have been much more difficult to recognize the logic without comparing Lao-tzu with these ancient philosophers. Now there is a common platform for these philosophies. Hopefully, our analysis can remove the artificial separation of East and West culture and let us have a more unified view of the world culture. East and West cultures are only two ways to seek the same human culture. We can understand a world culture, without wondering far from our own culture.[1]

---

[1] Chapter 47: "Without stepping outside the door, one may know the world." 不出於戶，以知天下。 We may also show that the principle is shared in our other humanistic efforts, such as in religions and psychology.

The logic model will also consolidate many approaches to deal with many common philosophical issues, such as appearance and reality, realism, idealism, phenomenology, and process philosophy. The logic can also be used to resolve many common dualism fallacies, such as "I and the world", "body and mind", "chicken and egg", and "white horse is not horse", and Zeno paradoxes, etc. These are issues of Ontology.

The Principle of Oneness

The logic of Tao philosophy is based on a clear principle. Although our discovery of the principle of Tao is completely unexpected, the principle is encoded with only a few Chinese characters in the first chapter of the *Tao Te Ching*.

In a short statement, the principle of Tao in Lao-tzu's teaching is a universal "Principle of Oneness." From the brevity and lucidness of his first Chapter, Lao-tzu's thought had reached its ultimate maturity when he wrote the principle as the first Chapter. I call this a universal view since this Principle is also the core of the early Greek philosophy, the Indian philosophy, and the Buddhist philosophers. It is also observed by modern philosophers and scientists.

We may state this principle simply as: every reality has Oneness; its true manifestations in the phenomenal world must have wholeness. Our thinking starts with dualistic objects, and this wholeness must be formed by the complementarity of the two dualistic objects.

The oneness of Tao is not a new idea. Many scholars in history have connected Tao with Oneness. For example, Wang Bi 王弼 (226–249 CE) says, "Although the *Tao Te Ching* has five thousand characters, what runs through them is Oneness." Chuang-tzu says, "The universe and I co-exist, and the myriad things and I are one." Hsu Sheng 許慎 (100 - 121 CE) says, "In the beginning, Tao establishes Oneness, from which we have heaven and earth, which evolves into the myriads. Everything from Oneness will follow Oneness." Chang Dai 張載 (1020 -1077 CE) also says, "The all-pervasive unity without any true duality." However, most of these assertions are brief and without detailed validation.

Our analytic results also reflect the views expressed by some Chinese philosophers. For example, Zhang Dongsun 張東蓀 labels Chinese logic as a "correlation logic," and Xiong Shili 熊十力 considers the ontological equivalence of all phenomenal manifestations of reality. Professor Wing-tsit Chan 陳榮捷 believes that we can introduce Western logic and science to consolidate Chinese metaphysics.

The logic of Tao philosophy deals with reality in general and is. Lao-tzu has applied this logic in various Chapters of the *Tao Te Ching* to describe the same principle of reality. The logic model is general and can be seen in many other fields, such as religion, psychotherapy, and science, etc.

Lao-tzu uses many examples in the Tao Te Ching to show this logic. He uses examples of describing the principle of Tao using dualistic objects. The most obvious one is the Principle of Complementarity.

As shown in this book, Lao-tzu's logic is clear and we have to clear him off all "absurdity." Previously we could not understand his logic is because we think in terms of language. Our logic model shows that a linguistic description of reality is always "vague, self-contradictory, and indeterminate." Lao-tzu's ambiguous language is unavoidable in the precise description of reality. It is only the language that is ambiguous; the reality itself is never ambiguous.

Therefore, we have to overcome the limits of linguistic description and search behind the ambiguous language for the truth. With this logic, we can avoid random speculations, but we are encouraged to speculate according to this principle of Tao.

The logic of the Principle of Oneness has an important consequence: Under a common ideal, our descriptions of the ideal may be different, but these descriptions should have an equivalent meaning. "The opposite of a truth is another truth." This is the basis of a plurality society.

Chapter VI Summary

Modern Sciences

Many traditional Tao scholars believe that Tao philosophy should *not* be analyzed with a scientific model because there is no logic in Tao philosophy. We have shown that such a belief is no longer valid and there is a definite logic structure in Tao philosophy. The logic is also consistent with modern sciences.

Basic human thinking is very similar in science and philosophy. Both search for the same unity of nature. Scientific thinking is based on the object level, where scientific theory binds together the objects and their interactions. The concept of Oneness is often embedded in the various "symmetry" properties or the conservation laws of scientific theory. Scientific progress is made when consolidations are achieved towards the Oneness of nature.

Sometimes, we sense many modern scientific ideas in Tao philosophy. It is now not surprising. In modern physics, we have a complementary duality of "particles and waves" and "space and time" in quantum theory and relativity, respectively. These theories all try to eliminate dualistic fragmentation. Our understanding of complementary models in science can help us re-orient our thinking about Tao philosophy. Both in science and philosophy, we may learn how to overcome the limits of language.

The mysteries of Tao philosophy and the mysteries of quantum theory have similar logic; they are due to the complementarity of dualistic opposite conceptual objects. Although modern sciences and Tao philosophy deal with different sets of objects, their basic principle is the same. Our model is consistent with the logical analysis of the method of physical theory.

The full symmetry of an absolute reality falls into two equivalent manifestations. This phenomenon is also similar to Spontaneous Symmetry Breaking in modern physics. The manifestations Heng Wu and Heng Yu obey identical principles, with an equal possibility to happen.

Religions

Many religions use gods to represent various principles in nature. In the *Tao Te Ching*, the holistic manifestation is also called god. In our logic discussion, god, Tao, and Nature all refer to the principle of Oneness.

In the logic of the basic Christian faith, the holistic manifestation of God is The Father, and the two manifestations of God are The Son and The Spirit. These three manifestations are ontologically equivalent. It constitutes a Trinity.

Chapter VI Summary

The teachings of Buddhism are summarized in the Middle Way, which identifies the Buddhist teachings as the Ultimate Truth and the Conventional Truth. The Ultimate Truth is at the Nirvana level, and the Conventional Truth is at the Samsara level. This is a dichotomy (Dualism) between the object level and the actuality level. The wholeness in Buddhism is represented as the un-fragmenting "Non-dualistic Way" (不二法門).

In the long development history of Indian religions, there are monotheism and polytheism. However, as shown in our model, these different religious teaching could be equivalent and are consistent with the logic principle of Oneness. For example, Indian Brahman has a Trinity manifestation. Brahma is the God who creates the myriad things; it represents the whole Brahman. Its two polarized manifestations are Shiva and Vishnu. Shiva is responsible for destruction, transformation, and regeneration, while Vishnu is the God who preserves the myriad things. Brahma, Shiva, and Vishnu form a Trinity.

A New Interpretation of Tao Te Ching

We must show that our model can interpret the *Tao Te Ching* with consistency. The *Tao Te Ching* is the best "experimental evidence" for our theory. If a new interpretation of the *Tao Te Ching* can indeed reflect the principle of Tao, then we may consider this model reasonable.

Traditional interpretations lack a central principle, so we wander among many possible meanings of each verse in the *Tao Te Ching,* and elaborate without bound. Now we have a clear logic principle, re-interpreting the *Tao Te Ching* becomes an important task. If we follow the principle, we will be able to see the proper meaning for each verse. Thus, we can have a more coherent interpretation.

We may analyze the chapters of the Tao Te Ching according to the principle of Tao discussed in this book. The most obvious one is the application of the principle of Complementarity in many chapters to overcome dualistic objects.

With a clear principle, translation of the *Tao Te Ching* into other languages will be less difficult. Translation of the *Tao Te Ching* has been difficult because the principle and logic have not been understood in the original text. Now, the original principle becomes is the *ultimate* goal of our translation. The principle can guide our thinking and compensate for linguistic differences.

In many scientific translations, many languages can be used to express the same principle without error. If we understand the principle to be translated, translation efforts become similar to what is required for a successful translation of a scientific theory.

I have published a separate translation under the title: *Tao Te Ching: An Ultimate Translation*.

A Paradigm Shift

This logic system is a new paradigm. Our model is a way to overcome Reductionism Fallacy. We have to change our habitual way of thinking. We need to avoid thinking in terms of objects and think in terms of the complementarity of the objects. So we can construct the reality of the actuality.

Therefore, comprehension of the logic of Tao philosophy will require a major paradigm shift. We use a detailed logic model to help us slowly adjust our thinking habits. This seems a formidable task. The mysteries of Tao can now be clarified on a logical platform. We can start to integrate our understanding of Tao philosophy into world philosophy. We should celebrate this achievement.

It will require a significant paradigm shift. The old paradigm will break down gradually while the new paradigm is established. However, the old paradigm has a very deep root and it will take persistence to bring about a change in our paradigm.

Appendix A: Trichotomy of Time

We expect that part-whole relation to behave with respect to time as it does with respect to space.

Theodore Sider
Four-Dimensionalism, p.87

The logic of dichotomy discussed in this book may be extended to our understanding of trichotomy or plurality. For example, our proper conceptual understanding of the trichotomy of time in terms of "past, present, and future" will directly affect our thinking about the meaning of life. The following discussion was presented at a conference by the author.

What is NOW?

How to live in Now has become an important topic in our discussion on life. A meaningful life often makes us feel that time is eternal. We often use "Living in Now" to mean that our life is meaningful at the moment.

We face a world with eternal changes, and often fall into anxiety and could not enjoy eternity. [1] We have to eliminate anxiety and let "Living in Now" manifest its meaning, and we can live in Now and feel "eternity and peace." A meaningful Now must be whole.

To completely "Live in Now" transcends the limits of Time and Space. In space, "Living in Now" transcends the dichotomy of "I and the World." In Time, "Living in Now" transcends the Trichotomy of "past, present, and future." To be able to "Live in Now" means that our life at present is meaningful and eternal.

Structure of Psychological Time

We habitually segregate time into past, present, and future. Such trichotomy breaks time into fragments, and thus induces an illusion about time. Fragments of "past, present, and future" are only concepts at the object level. We may call such objects the concepts of physical time.

---

[1] Anxiety is a fear without a clear subject. We have to analyze this anxiety into a fear with an object, so we can have courage, freedom, and creativity to deal with the fear and include the result into the life of Now.

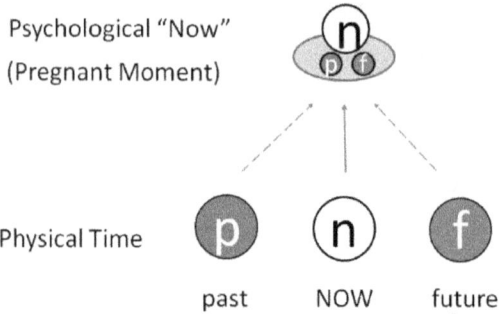

Figure 8 Psychological Time

In our discussion on the meaning of life, fragmentary physical time must be actualized to become a holistic and realistic perception of time. Realistic time is our direct apprehension of time, which may be called Psychological Time.[1] Following the Principle of Oneness, the structure of psychological time is that the past, present, and future must be superimposed to preserve the wholeness of time.

Past, Present, and Future have mutual influences. To make "Now" meaningful for our life, we have to evaluate our past and future positively in Now. *Now* may be changed by the new apprehension of our past; *Now* may also be influenced by our hope for the future. Therefore, a truthful NOW must reaffirm our past and hope for our future.

---

[1] In philosophy, there are also A-Theory (similar to Physical Time) and B-Theory (Similar to Psychological Time). Kierkegaard called such a psychological *now* a "Pregnant Moment." In B-Theory, past, present, and future are equally real.

Appendix B: Keyword

Holistic Changes in Time

A realistic NOW must be whole; therefore, its change must consist of the "unchanging," to be a whole. Therefore, "living in Now" is eternal, but is also ceaselessly changing.

According to our model, the real Now is entangled with "Past and Future" and forms a time packet. Such a time packet NOW can continue to exist ceaselessly, but its content is ceaselessly changing.

This time package flows as a whole, as shown in Figure 9.

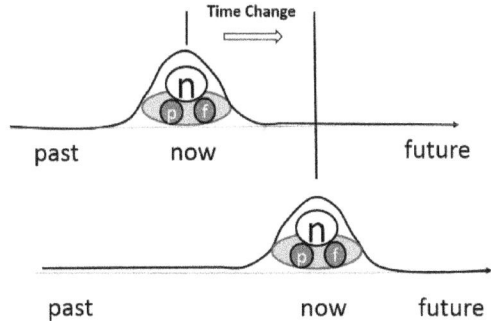

Figure 9 Time Change

This time packet NOW behaves like a *moving spotlight* to cover the whole life history in every moment of our life.

Such a time packet NOW can continue to exist ceaselessly, but its content is ceaselessly changing.[1] Only in such a "Now," we can maintain its identity with "changing-and-unchanging."

From such a time packet, limitless new things can appear in Now. Such creativity that preserves Oneness has flexibility and will maintain a holistic NOW. This is a concept of time that is consistent with the principle of Tao. Eternity or Heng is in Now.[2]

---

[1] Both East and West philosophy often describe a reality as "Becoming" and "Being". Such separation can easily fall into dualistic fallacies which regard Becoming as always changing and Being as always unchanging. A reality should transcend such dualistic view; a reality must cover Becoming and Being.

[2] According to Martin Heidegger we do not exist inside time, *we are time*. Hence, the relationship to the past is a present awareness of *having been*, which allows the past to exist in the present. The relationship to the future is the state of anticipating a potential possibility, task, or engagement. It is related to the human propensity for caring and being concerned, which causes "being ahead of oneself" when thinking of a pending occurrence. Therefore, this concern for a potential occurrence also allows the future to exist in the present. (Wikipedia, TIME)

Appendix B: Keywords

It is important to use the following definitions for the keywords used in our discussions of the principle and logic of Tao philosophy. These are the keywords used in Lao-tzu's description of the logic of Tao philosophy.

In the first chapter of the Tao Te Ching

- *Heng* (恆) - Heng means being whole or "holistic," so it can indicate a reality. Reality must be undivided; Heng covers the whole domain of reality. Heng is similar to Oneness and Wholeness in Greek philosophy. Heng may be translated as *true, persistent,* or *real* in our discussion.
- *Heng Tao* (恆道) is the holistic or true Tao. Heng Tao is the true order among the myriad things in nature.
- *Heng Name* (恆名) is a true description of the thing in nature. The true name describes the whole meaning of the thing, including its relationship to all other things in nature. Only such a name has reality.

- *Heng Yu* (恆有) is the *true* state of the myriad things when viewed as "differentiated," but the boundaries between the myriad things are disappearing to show their undifferentiation. Therefore, the state retains the wholeness nature of the myriad things. This is a whole state of dominant Yu comprising of some Wu.
- *Heng Wu* (恆無) is the *true* state of the myriad things when viewed as "undifferentiated", where the myriad things are subtly appearing as differentiated. It is a whole state of dominant Wu comprising of some Yu.
- *Name* (名) is a conventional name identifying an individual object. A name has "real" meaning only in the sub-domain of an object; it cannot represent a whole. Wu and Yu are examples of names.
- *Wu* (無) is defined as the state where the myriad things are completely undifferentiated. All things are treated without distinction and have no individual name.
- *Yu* (有) is defined as a state where myriad things are completely differentiated. All things are completely differentiated and assume individual names.

- *Obscurity* (玄) - is a state that cannot be described clearly with conventional names (language). It is a whole that shows all its parts at the same time, so it becomes "vague, self-contradictory, and indeterminate" characteristics of all its parts. The state cannot be clearly and distinctively described.

Keywords in the Logic Model

- *Absolute Reality* or *Reality* is the reality under investigation. It has a definite whole domain and all realist manifestations of this reality must cover the same domain. An Absolute Reality has no characteristics other than Oneness. In Tao philosophy, this reality is the nature of the myriad things. The basic reality of the myriad things is the Oneness of all.
- *Phenomenal World* – The manifestations of absolute reality are phenomena with characteristics in nature. The phenomenal world refers to where we identify phenomena with names. We may identify the phenomena with *objects* or *manifestations*. The objects can describe the manifestations, which are also named.
- *Manifestations of Tao* or *Actualities* are the true nature of the myriad things in the phenomenal world. The true nature reflects the principle of absolute reality in the phenomenal world. Heng Wu and Heng Yu are the Actualities or the True Manifestations of Tao. Our linguistic description of these manifestations (in terms of the objects) will always appear obscure.

- ***Objects*** are names we designate for the myriad things in the phenomenal world. Each object describes a sub-domain of reality. These objects become our shared knowledge that has been encoded as part of our language. Therefore, objects are dualistic and are with segmented names that are used in our communication of reality.
- ***Interactions/Correlations*** of the objects are postulated between the objects to reconnect the objects back into a whole. The objects are parts of the whole. The purpose of these interactions is to *harmonize* the objects to regain wholeness to form actualities to describe the manifestations.
- ***Oneness*** means that all things are One. Oneness has no characteristics other than perfect symmetry. Absolute Reality is in the state of Oneness. Oneness covers the whole domain without any differentiation.
- ***Wholeness*** means the whole domain of reality. Reality must be a whole; every being (reality) must cover the same domain, i.e., to have wholeness. In Tao philosophy, wholeness is Heng, so Heng Tao, Heng Wu, and Heng Yu are realistic descriptions of the nature of the myriad things.

Appendix B: Keyword

- *The Principle of Oneness* states that the true manifestations of reality may have different characteristics and must appear at the same time. Each manifestation can independently represent the same reality. All realistic descriptions must be whole, to represent the Oneness.
- *Te (Principle of Tao)* is the law or principle of interactions that preserve the harmonious relationship among the myriad things. Te reflects the principle of Tao in the phenomenal world. We describe the myriad things in terms of objects, so Te is the principle of interactions of all objects. Each object must follow its Te to be harmonious with all others. Te is the way to ensure the Principle of Oneness is observed.
- *Non-duality* means Oneness or Wholeness. We often think or describe in terms of dualistic objects, but they can be harmonized to form actualities that are non-dualistic. The manifestations are non-dualistic. *Dualism/Duality* refers to two opposite objects that constitute a whole. In our model, the dual objects are complementary.

- ***Ontological Equivalence*** – The manifestations of Tao are equivalent representations of Tao, so they have ontological equivalence in representing reality. Each manifestation is designated as an actuality in the model. Two actualities or manifestations (Heng Wu and Heng Yu) of Tao are dual representations of the same Tao. Ontology is related to reality. The manifestations are Parallel Realities.
- ***Complementarity*** states that (in quantum theory) wave and particle properties must complement each other in describing a quantum reality. In our model, two objects (parts), Wu and Yu, must complement each other to account for the whole manifestations (Heng Wu and Heng Yu) of Tao. Wu and Yu cannot be fully described without including the opposite state. This means that Wu and Yu are always in a complementary state in reality.
- ***Entanglement*** – When a reality without polarization (Heng Tao) becomes (decays into) two polarized manifestations (Heng Wu and Heng Yu), then Heng Wu and Heng Yu are in the state of entanglement.

Other Keywords

- ***Worm Holes*** are two-way connections from one part of the universe to another part of the same universe very quickly or would allow travel from one universe to another. If Heng Wu and Heng Yu are two parts of the same universe, they are connected through the two eyes of the Tai-ji Symbol.
- ***Trinity*** – Two manifestations and absolute reality refer to the same truth. The two manifestations appear simultaneously and represent the same reality. For example, body and soul are two manifestations of spirit.
- ***The Doctrine of Two Truths*** – The two manifestations of reality is equivalent truths. The manifestations represent the same reality.

References

Adler (1985)	Adler, Mortimer J., " Ten Philosophical Mistakes," MacMillan, 1985. P.xix.
Ames (2003)	Ames, Roger, and Hall, David, *Dao De Jing: A Philosophical Translation*, Ballantine Books (2003)
Chan (1963)	Chan, Wing-Tsit, *The Way of Lao Tzu* (Tao-te ching). New York. The Bobbs-Merrill Company. P.97.
Duhem (1991)	Duhem, Pierre, *The Aim and Structure of Physical Theory*, Princeton University Press, 1991.
French (1985)	Wheeler, John A., *Physics in Copenhagen in 1934 and 1935*, in *Niels Bohr: A Centenary Volume*, Ed. By A.P. French and P.J. Kennedy, Harvard University Press. P. 224.
Guenon (2004)	Guenon, Rene, *The Multiple States of the Being*, Sophia Perennis, 2004
Kosko (1994)	Kosko, Bart, *Fuzzy Thinking*, Flamingo, New York (1994)
Plotnitsky (1994)	Plotnitsky, Artady, *Complementarity*, Duke University Press, p.5 (1994)
Putnam (1981)	Putnam, Hilary, *Reason, Truth and History*, Cambridge University Press (1981).
Putnam (1987)	Putnam, Hilary, *The Many Faces of Realism*, Open Court, (1987)

Popper (1978)	Popper, Karl, *Three Worlds*, The Tanner Lecture on Human Values, Delivered at The University of Michigan, April 7, 1978.
Tong (2001)	Tong, Lik Kuen, "*The Art of Appropriation: Towards a Field-Being Concept of Philosophy*," International Journal of Field Being, vol.1 (1), Part 1, 2001.
Wang (2000)	Wang, (James) Qingjie (2000). Heng Dao and Appropriation of Nature - A Hermeneutical Interpretation of Laozi. Asian Philosophy, 10(2), 149-163. "Heng and Temporality of Dao: Laozi and Heidegger," in Dao: A Journal of Comparative Philosophy, vol.1, no.1, pp.55-71.
Wang (2004)	Wang, Wayne L., *Dynamic Tao, and Its Manifestations*, Helena Island Publisher, Darien, Illinois 2004. ISBN 0-9727496-0-8.
Wang (2006)	Wang, Wayne L., *A Basic Theory of Tao Philosophy*, International Conference on Taoism, May 6-7, 2006 Taipei, Taiwan.
Wang (2012)	Wang, Wayne L., "道家哲學的邏輯 *(The Logic of Tao Philosophy)*", in the *Tamkang Journal of Humanities and Social Sciences* (淡江人文社會學刊), Vol. 49 (2012), pp. 1-32.
Wang (2013)	Wang, Wayne L., *Tao Te Ching: An Ultimate Translation*, Amazon Kindle Book and Paperback, Helena Island Publisher, Darien, Illinois (2013) ISBN 978-09727496-2-6.
Whitehead (1978)	Whitehead, Alfred North, *Process and Reality*, New York, The Free Press,

INDEX

Absolute Reality, 27, 143
actuality level, 27
Actuality 實象, 122, 143
actualization process, 57
Aristotle, 87
Asian Thoughts, 10
Basic Theory of Tao Philosophy, 5, 53, 150, 155
Becoming, 112
being, 75, 112
Being, 46, 75
beings, 96
Book of Change 易經, 1
Book of Tao and Te, 52
Borderless 徼, 25
Bradley, v
Brain, 69
Buddhism, 7, 31, 126
Chang Dai 張載, 128
Chapter 1, 17
Chi 氣, 85, 86
Chuang-tzu 莊子, 76, 103, 122, 128
Complementarity, 29, 45, 49, 86, 131
Complex Concept, 39, 60
Conceptual Relation, vi
Conceptual Relationship, 42
Cyclic Transition, 48
Derrida, 2
Difference, 24
Division 曲, 114
Doctrine of Two Truths, 29, 78, 79
Domain, Whole, 19, 144
Dualistic Fallacy, 93
Dynamic Tao and Its Manifestations, 5

Enumeration 數, 121
Epistemological Pluralism, 122
Expectation Value, 62
Field, 86
Fuzzy Logic, 64, 66
Ghost 鬼, 74
God 神, 74, 121
Gongsun Long 公孫龍, 2, 111
Grand System of Tao, 104
Grand System 大制, 105
Greek Philosophy, 31, 126, 140
Guodian 郭店, 100
Han Yin 韓嬰, 103
Hegel, 2
Heng Name 恆名, 19, 27, 140
Heng Tao 恆道, 19, 21, 140
Heng Wu 恆無, 20, 24, 45, 141
Heng Yu 恆有, 20, 24, 45, 141
Heng 恆, 21, 140
Heraclitus, 52, 109, 126
Hilary Putnam, 123
Hinduism, 7
Hsu Sheng 許慎, 128
Hsuen-tzu 荀子, 2, 88, 122
Hu Shih 胡適, 3
Hui-shi 惠施, 2
Idea 意, 121
Indeterminate, vii
Interaction Model, vi, 38, 39, 43
Interference, 49, 62
Jin Yuelin 金玉霖, 3, 122
Kant, v
Knowledge 智, 115
Law of Interactions 德, 85
Li 禮, 119

Linguistic Model, vi, 38, 43, 45, 50, 64
Liu Heng 劉恆, 21
Logic of Tao philosophy, 70
Logic of Tao Philosophy, viii, 25, 37, 61, 65, 150
Logic of Tao Philosophy., 4
Logical Truth, 32
Manifestation, v, 143
Many-Worlds, 58
Mawangdui 馬王堆, 17, 21
Mereological Principle, 67
Mo-tzu 墨子, 2
Nagarjuna, 79, 126
Name 名, 27, 122, 141
Niels Bohr, 55
Non-duality, 7, 143, 145
Non-duality Principle, 126
Non-polarization, 74
Now, 135
object level, 27
Object 物象, 20, 80, 144
Objectification, 79
Objects 器, 121
obscurity, 26
Obscurity 玄, 21, 142
Oneness, 30
Oneness 一, iv, 13
Ontological Equivalence, 26, 29, 128, 146
Ontological Ground, 75
Ontological Truth, 32
ontologically equivalent, 29
Paradigm Shift, 76
Parallel Realities, 146
Parallel Universe, 55
Parmenides, v, 79, 96, 126
Parts and the Whole, 90
Perennial Philosophy, 10
Perturbation Theory, 116
Phenomenal World, 143

Philosophy of Nature, iv, 23
Philosophy of Oneness, 7
Philosophy of Organism, 120, 121
Physical time, 136
Plato, v
Plotinus, v
Pluralistic Epistemology, 58
Popper, Karl, 66
Power of Tao, 52
Pre-Socratic, 7
Principle of Complementarity, iv, 25, 30, 46
Principle of Equivalence, iv, 26, 30, 48, 76, 77, 78
Principle of Interactions 德, 48
Principle of Interactions 德, 52
Principle of Oneness, 22, 30, 76
Principle of Oneness 恆一原則, 7, 120, 145
Principle of Oneness 恆一法則, iv
Principle of Ontological Parity, 26
Principle of Tao, ii, iv, 15, 91, 102, 145
Process Philosophy, 99, 116
Profound Te 玄德, 85
Profoundness 玄, 65
Psychological Time, 137
Quantum Theory, 107
Realism, 149
reality vectors, 56
Reality Vectors, 57
Relational Proposition, 47
Ren 仁, 119
Sameness, 24
Schelling, v
Science, v, 5, 8, 13, 128, 134
Self-Contradiction, vii, 64, 99
Shao Yong 邵雍, 121
Simple Concept, 39, 60
Softness, 111
Spirit 精, 74

Index 索引

state function, 62
Subcontrary Opposites, 32
Subtlety 妙, 25
superposition, 45
Superposition, 49, 60
Symbols 象, 121
Tai-ji 太極, 53
Te 德, 52, 85, 119, 120
Teaching with No Word 不言之教, 90
teleological, 42
Teleological Force, 87
Tenderness, 111
The First Principle, 125
The Way of Wu, 115
The Way of Yu, 115
Third World, 65
Thought Space, 56
Three World Logic, 66
Three Worlds, 66
Time, 113
Tong, Lik-kuen, 26
Trichotomy, 135
Trinity, 75, 78, 117
Tung Chung-shu 董仲舒, 103
Ultimate Polarization 太極, 54

Vague, vii
Valley 谷, 74
Wang Bi 王弼, 17, 101, 121, 128
Wen-tzu 文子, 121
Whitehead, A. N., v, 116, 121
Wholeness, 111, 140
Wing-tsit Chan 陳榮捷, 128
Wing-tsit Chan 陳榮捷, 16
Wisdom 知, 115
Words 言, 60, 121
Wu 無, 20, 24, 141
Wu-wei 無爲, 90, 102, 115
Xiong Shili 熊十力, 128
Yan Fu 嚴復, 3
Yang 陽, 86
Yi 義, 119
Yi-Chuan 易傳, 74
Yi-Chuang 易傳, 54
Yin 陰, 86
Yu 有, 20, 24, 141
Yu-wei 有爲, 102
Zhang Dongsun 張東蓀, 3, 58, 122, 128
一陰一陽之謂道, 54

ABOUT THE AUTHOR

Wayne L. Wang has been an independent researcher on Tao philosophy since 1999. He became interested in Tao philosophy because *Tao Te Ching* has been treated as a mysterious philosophy, but shows some similarities to scientific phenomena.

His first analysis was published as *The Dynamic Tao and its Manifestations* (2004). He has since devoted his time to further clarification of the principle of Tao philosophy. He has surveyed and consolidated many ancient and modern philosophies and formulated a consistent logic model for Tao philosophy.

He has published The Basic Theory of Tao Philosophy (2006), which shows an initial scientific model reflecting the Tai-ji relationship in Tao. He first published a complete logic structure in a Chinese article The Logic of Tao Philosophy (2012). The model and its application are summarized in two books: *The Logic of Tao Philosophy (2013)* and *Tao Te Ching: An Ultimate Translation* (2013). In 2014, he applied the logic of Tao philosophy and incorporate psychotherapy, religion, and Western philosophy in his first book in Chinese 尋求人生的意義 (*Searching for the Meaning of Life*). These works represent a major milestone in his search for the foundation of Tao philosophy. It makes a logical and self-consistent translation possible.

He holds a Ph. D. degree from M. I. T. and resides near Chicago, Illinois, USA. Please send your comments and suggestions to:

email: wwwang@alum.mit.edu.
Website: http://www.dynamictaos.com/